NEW MAINERS ✦ *Portraits of Our Immigrant Neighbors*

NEW MAINERS

Portraits of Our Immigrant Neighbors

Photographs by Jan Pieter van Voorst van Beest

Text by Pat Nyhan

Foreword by Reza Jalali

Tilbury House, Publishers
Gardiner, Maine

TILBURY HOUSE, PUBLISHERS
103 Brunswick Avenue, Gardiner, Maine 04345
800–582–1899 • www.tilburyhouse.com

First paperback edition: March 2009
10 9 8 7 6 5 4 3 2 1

Library of Congress Cataloging-in-Publication Data

Voorst van Beest, Jan Pieter van, 1944-
New Mainers : portraits of our immigrant neighbors / Jan Pieter van Voorst van Beest ; text by Pat Nyhan ; foreword by Reza Jalali. — 1st pbk. ed.
       p. cm.
   Includes bibliographical references.
   ISBN 978-0-88448-312-0 (alk. paper)
1. Ethnology—Maine—Pictorial works. 2. Immigrants—Maine—Portraits.
3. Minorities—Maine—Portraits. 4. Maine—Ethnic relations—Pictorial works.
5. Immigrants—Maine—Biography. 6. Minorities—Maine—Biography.
7. Maine—Biography. 8. Maine—Ethnic relations. I. Nyhan, Patricia. II. Title.
   F30.A1V66 2009
   304.8'7410090511—dc22   2008050251

Cover photographs by Jan Pieter van Voorst van Beest
Front cover fabric detail is from a men's weave, Akan/Ashanti, Ghana, Catalog No. 90.1/9409, courtesy of the Division of Anthropology, American Museum of Natural History
Designed by Geraldine Millham, Westport, Massachusetts
Copyediting by Genie Dailey, Fine Points Editorial Services, Jefferson, Maine
Printed and bound by Maple Vail, Kirkwood, New York.

To the new immigrants who have so enriched life in Maine.

CONTENTS

Acknowledgments   ix

Preface   xi

Foreword   xiii

Introduction   xxiii

NEW MAINERS ✛ *Portraits of Our Immigrant Neighbors*

CHAPTER 1	Hooria Majeed, Afghanistan	1
CHAPTER 2	Jose Castaneda, El Salvador	7
CHAPTER 3	Khadija Guled, Somalia	13
CHAPTER 4	Amarpreet and Hermeet Kohli, India	19
CHAPTER 5	Makara Meng, Cambodia	25
CHAPTER 6	Shamou, Iran	31
CHAPTER 7	Mary Otto, Sudan	37
CHAPTER 8	Gerard Kiladjian, Syria	43
CHAPTER 9	Grace Valenzuela, Philippines	49
CHAPTER 10	Oscar Mokeme, Nigeria	55
CHAPTER 11	Van and Kim Luu, Vietnam	61
CHAPTER 12	Zeynep Turk, Turkey	67
CHAPTER 13	Emrush Zeqiri, Kosovo	73
CHAPTER 14	Rifat and Tasneem Zaidi, Pakistan	79
CHAPTER 15	Winston Williams, Jamaica	85
CHAPTER 16	Suwanna Sanguantonkallaya, Thailand	91
CHAPTER 17	Rafael Galvez, Peru	95
CHAPTER 18	Jaden Li Eung, Cambodia	101
CHAPTER 19	Abdullah Pious Ali, Ghana	107
CHAPTER 20	Lana Shkolnik and Galina Antonovskiy, Russia	113
CHAPTER 21	Tomas Fortson, Mexico	119
CHAPTER 22	Ismail Ahmed, Somalia	125
CHAPTER 23	Laura Val, Romania	131
CHAPTER 24	Timwah Luk, Hong Kong	137
CHAPTER 25	Jelilat Oyetunji, Nigeria	143
APPENDIX	A Look at Recent Immigration in Maine	149
	About the Authors	156

ACKNOWLEDGMENTS

This book is the result of a close collaboration between the authors and Reza Jalali. Without Reza's dedication and deep knowledge of the immigrant community in Maine we would not have been able to complete the project. He contacted and arranged for us to meet with most of the people we photographed and interviewed.

We also want to thank Jennifer Bunting at Tilbury House, Publishers, for giving us the opportunity to tell these stories. It is good to have a publisher in Maine who dares to take on important, sometimes controversial, issues.

We gratefully acknowledge all the people in this book for sharing their amazing experiences with us. We deeply appreciate their cooperation and hospitality, inviting us to their homes or places of work and spending extended time with us. We feel honored to have been able to work with them, and we hope that our "portraits" do them justice.

Thanks also to Rafael Galvez for interpreting services, and to Phil Nadeau, deputy city administrator, City of Lewiston; Regal Naseef; Abraham Peck, University of Southern Maine; Juan Perez-Febles, state monitor advocate, Migrant & Immigrant Services, Maine Department of Labor; Beth Stickney, executive director, Immigrant Legal Advocacy Project; Robert Wood, co-director, Portland Adult Education; Karen Zuckerman; the teachers of English as a Second Language at Portland Adult Education; and the University of Southern Maine's Office of Multicultural Student Affairs.

Finally, we want to thank our spouses, Andrea and Chris, and Reza's wife, Jaleh, who patiently supported us in this endeavor.

This book came about because we wanted to get to know our new neighbors better. With immigrants from so many different countries changing the face of our state in recent years, we set out to find out who they are, what their lives were like before they moved here, why they came, and how they are experiencing life in Maine. We wrote this book to welcome and honor them, and to help raise awareness about them in our communities.

By "new Mainers," we mean immigrants who came here in the past thirty years or so who are from different countries than those from which immigrants came in the past, such as England, Ireland, Italy, and French-speaking Canada. We used a very broad definition of "immigrants" as people who came from other countries and are part of the fabric of Maine life, whether they moved here voluntarily, or were resettled as refugees, or are migrant workers. We sought a sampling by gender, age, occupation, religion, country of origin, and reason for immigrating. The mix we wound up with in no way represents a complete picture, but rather highlights the main regions of the world from which these new Mainers come.

It was not easy for the people included here to tell their stories. Some refugees are still struggling to adjust to their new lives or want to put the pain of their past lives behind them. Immigrants who moved here voluntarily for a better economic life, or because Maine is a small, safe environment in which to raise a family, may have had an easier passage, but still confront issues of leaving behind family, language, and a way of life. It can be hard to put into words what one feels about such deeply personal issues.

We encouraged the immigrants to present themselves on their own terms, both visually in the photos and orally through the interviews on which their stories are based. We made little attempt to fact-check their stories beyond researching relevant places and events. Nor did we "correct" occasional imperfect grammar, since the speech of someone still new to English is worth no less than a native speaker's and it has its own richness of expression. The immigrants' stories in this book are their stories, told largely in their own words.

FOREWORD
by Reza Jalali

We may have come in different ships, but we're all in the same boat now.
—Martin Luther King, Jr.

In my extended family there is a tale going back to my childhood in Kurdistan, Iran. Like many good stories, it begins with a knock at the door. My mother, carrying me, the youngest of her nine children, answers it to find a group of singing gypsy women. One of them offers to tell her fortune in exchange for money. Curious, Khanum, as we called Mother, stretches one hand out while holding on to me tight, for the common myth was that gypsies—the wandering "refugees" since ancient times—snatched city babies to raise them as their own. The gypsy loses interest in reading Khanum's palm and instead peeks at my face and sighs.

"Your baby shall drink much water in strange lands," the woman says in her broken Farsi, her face turning pale, for she knows such news could mean less reward. Upset on hearing her youngest child might move to a faraway land to live among strangers, Khanum curses the unfortunate woman and throws some change at her before shutting the door. Still grasping me, she weeps, unmoved by my grandmother's pleas that tears of such bitterness would sour her breast milk.

Growing up in a small town on the border of Iran and Iraq, Qasre-Shirin (the Palace of Shirin), named so in honor of the tragic love affair of the Armenian queen Shirin and a poor stonecutter, Farhad, I heard the story of the gypsy's visit again and again. Yet every time I listened to this family tale, I felt a fresh sadness, as heavy as the nearby mountains where the stonecutter had hacked at the rocks, day and night, to show his unfulfilled love for the beautiful queen.

As time went by and the world around us transformed, I began to sense a premonition in Khanum's eyes whenever we were alone together. By the time I was in high school, the Shah's secret police, SAVAK, were arresting young Iranians, Kurds or not, as the antigovernment opposition grew inside and outside of Iran. Fearful for my safety, I left Iran to go to India to pursue my studies while waiting for the fall of the U.S.-backed Shah Mohammad Reza Pahlavi's regime. Naïve and young, I pictured my return to a new Iran, democratic and tolerant of minorities, in a few years.

The much-anticipated Iranian revolution came in 1979, when the population tired of the regime's tyranny and corruption and, seduced by the promises of a white-bearded old ayatollah, forced the Shah to flee the country. The promised liberty for all, equity, and democracy did not materialize, and in the post-revolution period which followed, I, like countless other Iranians living and studying outside of Iran who had been active in the Iranian political scene, became a stateless person. To make things worse, in 1980 the Iran-Iraq War started. In the years to follow, living in Bangalore, India, under the protection of the United Nations High Commissioner for Refugees (UNHCR), I followed the news of the war and the destruction of my birthplace, the city of lovers, with a heartache that would become a permanent companion in my new life as a man without a country.

In 1985, my application to be admitted to the U.S. as a political refugee was accepted. Without a sponsor—I knew no one in the U.S.—I was sent to Portland, Maine, to be settled. In my new life in Portland, sitting in my apartment, once again I followed the news of the war until it ended in 1988. To my surprise, the taking and retaking of the towns and villages on both sides of the border, such as Qasre-Shirin, by the Iranian and Iraqi armies would rarely make it to the pages of the local newspaper. It seemed, as far as most Americans were concerned, this war was someone else's headache.

By then, most of my family, including Khanum, displaced by the ongoing war, had moved away to safer parts of Iran. Unable to visit them there, every few years I would save enough money to fly to Istanbul, Turkey, to rendezvous with them.

During one such visit, Khanum offered to retell the gypsy's story. As I listened and watched her eyes grow moist, feeling guilty, I lied, "Things will change and I will move back to Iran to live near you."

Though she knew better, she wiped her tears and said, "Insha'ullah [God willing]."

A decade later, I am still ashamed of my words of betrayal, since in a few years she passed away in Iran.

That I have lived outside of Kurdistan for more than thirty years, never to return save a few brief visits, is a reminder of life's cruelty. Robert Frost said that every poem begins with a knot in the throat. So does describing a life spent in exile, voluntarily or not—the loneliness of life among the unfamiliar, survival in the "no-man's land," the in-betweenness, the search for identity, and the regret one feels when remembering home.

Displaced people and other immigrants live a life marked by longing for belonging, and a faint hope, fading as time passes, that one day the return to "home" will become a possibility. Years after my mother passed away, I wrote of her longing as a "refugee," displaced in her own country, in an essay for the *Maine Sunday*

Telegram: "Recently, my mother had started to wear a key around her neck. It was the key to our ancestor's house, which was lost and ultimately destroyed during the long Iran-Iraq War. She wore the key to remind herself and the rest of us what we had lost to the war." I suspected, in her case, just like the Jewish shopkeeper forced out of Poland, or the Palestinian farmer chased away from his ancestral home, holding a key to a past which no longer existed was to stay connected, however remotely, to that former world.

My introduction to the plight of displaced people came when I was young. One summer, our dusty Kurdish border town became the arrival point for Iraqi Jewish refugees, forced out of a country where they had lived for centuries. They came in buses and lorries looking tired and anxious. Curious, I went to watch them arrive. There was a family with children my age. We did not speak each other's languages, but I could see the fear in their eyes. Some settled down in border towns such as Qasre-Shirin, perhaps thinking they would be back in Iraq in no time. Most of them remained to live among us, learning Kurdish and Farsi, working and starting new families in a city without a synagogue. In the years that followed, other Iraqi refugees, Kurds and Shia Muslims, came in larger numbers.

As a Kurd, being displaced and stateless is in my DNA. My own father, an Azeri, was sent to Kurdistan by his father to search for his brother who, on a pilgrimage to the holy city of Karbala in Iraq, had left Azerbaijan only to disappear without a trace. My father, then a young man, along with a cousin of the same age, was given a handful of silver coins and a silk rug to exchange for money should there be an emergency, and sent on a mission which ended in failure. My father did not go back; he and the cousin married two beautiful Kurdish women and started their own families.

Too ashamed to return to his family, my father stayed away from Azerbaijan for more than forty years. Once, in his sixties, and a confident and wise dervish (Muslim mystic) by then, he decided to visit "home." He took me along as we went searching for the people he had left behind. We met old men and women he had played with as children. I recall watching the heartfelt scenes and making a promise—which of course I failed to keep—to never leave "home." Even while studying in India, I dreamed of going back to Qasre-Shirin to live, to marry a Kurdish woman and raise sons and daughters in a town known near and far for its starry nights and crisscrossing river. Instead, I ended up in Maine as a stateless single man.

I arrived in Portland from India on Memorial Day weekend in 1985. I still remember the flags displayed everywhere. President Ronald Reagan was loathed by many outside the U.S. for his unconditional support of the warlords in Afghanistan.

Until then I had assumed the American public to be well informed and politically engaged. I was disappointed to hear many of my co-workers worrying about the Celtics games rather than the disturbing news that the U.S. had been secretly selling arms to the ayatollahs in Iran and using the profits to finance the Contras in Nicaragua. Similarly, few seemed to care that the Iraqi dictator Saddam Hussein was being armed by the U.S. in his war against the Iranians. By the 1990s, "Saddam" would become a household name in the U.S.

Still, once I got to Portland, my new "home," it felt like a sweet dream. To my tired eyes, the electric light seemed brighter and the sky looked bluer. I would walk around—penniless, single and without a friend—enjoying the new sights and sounds. With the curiosity of a lost traveler, I would watch people around me. My eyes would light up like a baby's when I caught a glimpse of the ocean. Lost in the narrow streets of the city's West End, I would stop to admire the magically fragrant lilac bushes leaning over the fences. Open-mouthed, with my head tilted back, I would chase with my eyes the birds whose English names I was yet to learn as they took flight into the New England sky. Feeling alive with excitement, I would marvel at the openness with which pretty women flirted with me. At times like these, I felt, after years of searching, I had found a home.

If leaving one's home is like a death, settling down in a new country is like a rebirth. Like a baby, one learns by watching others, making mistakes, crying and laughing when provoked. It took me a while to realize not every gaze was friendly—although I must admit I was a sight to stare at. Although most people around me dressed in shorts and T-shirts, baring pale flesh, I was dressed in layers of sweaters, for Maine's early June temperatures of low sixties felt intolerably cold compared to India's heat.

Weeks later, as I walked down Congress Street gazing into store windows and walking inside just to look at the merchandise, I felt unwelcome. At one clothing store known for its low prices, I was followed around by the unfriendly store manager. When I pretended to be interested in a fleece jacket, he wanted to know if I could afford it. For a long time afterwards, every time I passed that store I had a maddening urge to throw a rock through its plate-glass windows.

Though I had come to accept the fact that most New Englanders were aloof, I still felt sad whenever a pair of cold blue eyes stared at me as if questioning my right to be here in Maine. Soon, doubts started to form in my head. In the privacy of my damp, tiny apartment on Danforth Street, staring at the bathroom mirror, I searched for a clue. It must be my Middle-Eastern look, I said to myself. So I shaved off my mustache! In years to follow, I would shed layers of my cultural coverings, consciously or not, and become wary of my accent and hide my true feelings, all in order to fit in. I told myself this was going to be "home" irrespective of my discomforts and loneliness.

As I started to look for jobs, I realized my university degree from India was treated with suspicion. My Muslim name did not help either. As an outsider, I was ignorant of the social codes and the norms. It would be years before I learned what Moxie was and how the fiddlehead could be cooked!

I started to avoid two groups of people. One group was those who, perhaps more out of ignorance than malice, would congratulate me for having made it out of the Middle East, as if the region had been hit with plague. I would smile back and say nothing rather than explain that I still had ties with the region and my loved ones still lived there. The other group would look at me with pity, as if being a refugee meant one was dumb. These people would speak to me slowly but loudly, perhaps thinking my not knowing good English was due to a hearing deficiency, or they would explain the working of a faucet in the way a grownup speaks to a child.

When the first Gulf War started, Islamophobia surfaced and flag-waving Americans found their targets in peaceful Muslims or Arabs living in the U.S. In 1992, in an airport in Texas, I was pulled out of a plane on its way to Costa Rica by the airport manager, citing "security concern." When I worked as a social worker at the Augusta Mental Health Institute, one day on my way to work I stopped for gas in a small town and was chased out of the station by the angry owner.

"We don't sell gas to f——ing Arabs!" he yelled threateningly.

I started to laugh, which only made him more upset. "But I'm not even an Arab!" I muttered as I walked back to my car to leave.

Another time, a man standing with his friends smoking outside a bar looked at me and yelled, "Go back!" I walked away, pretending I did not hear him but imagining everyone else in the street did. I felt ashamed of my cowardice and recoiled in humiliation. But in my head I yelled back saying how much I *wanted* to go "back" if only I could. Xenophobia knows no logic. While I was working at Portland's welfare department, a homeless veteran ran out of my office angrily demanding to be seen by someone else, for he would not have a "Russian" caseworker look at his record!

Gradually, perhaps unconsciously in agreement with Descartes that "When living in the midst of others, do not stand out too much," I felt and acted invisible as I tiptoed through crowds in streets, malls, fairs, and cinemas, unseen and unspoken to, like a ghost. During holidays I felt homesick and lonely. I could not, try as I might, share in the joy of the loud laughter and the celebration that went on around me. During one New Year's Eve celebration, as I stood watching the fireworks explode overhead in the black December sky, my toes freezing in my cheap boots, I realized I knew nobody in the large crowd gathered to welcome the arrival of another year. As the crowd screamed every time the sky glittered with millions of tiny colorful sparks, it dawned on me that I was alone in a city of thousands and in a country of millions. I rushed home feeling terrified.

During darker times, inside my apartment, I faced ghosts who would show up uninvited to remind me of times I had spent in Indian police stations and jails for my peaceful political activities opposing the Iranian government, and of friends and classmates who had died in Iranian prisons.

In a factory in South Portland where I worked the graveyard shift in order to attend classes at the university during the day, I was taunted by some co-workers. Some were unhappy with me as I publicly voiced my opposition to the slaughter of Iraqi civilians during the Gulf War in an interview with the local newspaper.

"If you don't like it here, go back to your camels," a man cried from a nearby table as I was sitting down for a cafeteria meal during the 3:00 A.M. break and wondering if it counted for dinner or breakfast. I ignored him and faked a new interest in what was on the plastic plate in front of me. Next, I heard a woman laughing. A tape ran inside my head, like an old movie—a tray smashed on my head, chairs thrown around, the security guards taking me outside, and next day a manager firing me from a job which paid for my rent, food, and part of my university tuition. The corn kernels turned into coarse sands inside my mouth. I was tired and on edge; here I was back at work after a twelve-hour shift the day before and catching a few hours of sleep and attending a class in between. I stabbed the boiled corncob on my plate with the steel knife and sat there wanting to scream. Hidden under the metal dining table, my knees were shaking. I waited for everyone to leave before standing up to empty my tray. Later, alone in the bathroom stall, I wept and cursed. I took a pen out of my blue factory-issued coat and wrote on the wall, "I hate my life."

But it was in the same Maine that I witnessed, again and again, the grace, the kindness, and the generosity for which most Americans and Mainers are known. Most often such kindness would wrap itself around me, the way the morning fog embraced the islands on Casco Bay in wintertime. On the day I arrived at the airport in Portland, Sam and Sandy offered to take me to their home in Cape Elizabeth. Years later, when Sandy was diagnosed with cancer at the same time as one of my sisters living in Iran was, I found myself praying for them both—two sisters living in two different worlds. Sandy survived her illness, but my sister, Porun, did not. Rana, who volunteered at the local refugee resettlement agency, drove me to job interviews and helped me find a place to live. Selma and Hershy, the Brunswick peacemakers, and Jack, the Irishman in charge of Amnesty International USA for years, and countless other moral giants all taught me why it was important to "break the silence."

It was in Portland when my co-workers at the welfare department surprised me with a cake made to look like an American flag the day I became a naturalized citizen. In Maine, I bought my first home, signing the papers with a knot in my throat, knowing my parents would never see it. It was at the Portland Club where I danced with my wife like a crazed dervish when we celebrated our marriage with friends. With the year's first snow falling silently on bare trees outside a medical building, I heard, for the first time, the heartbeat of our son, Azad ("the one who is free"). During the darkest time of my life, when chained to a wall in a prison cell in Bangalore, India, in order to stay sane I had dreamed of having a son one day and naming him Azad. In fields in the suburbs of Portland, I got to coach our son's and daughter's soccer teams, seeing myself in them as they ran around kicking the ball. In basements of churches and in school gyms, I got to vote, a privilege and right I had never been given before.

It is in Maine that I have felt safe and confident enough to write again; to speak before crowds, whether at Harvard University or in a rally in Washington, D.C.; to attend a meeting at the White House to address human-rights concerns; to be a guest on *Oprah;* to once again to become a Muslim and read poetry (two essential requirements for becoming a dervish); and to finally dream again. Now, I laugh louder and weep softer.

Once, a single mother, a client at the welfare office where I worked, showed up at my office to drop a few wrinkled dollars and some change on my desk.

"I've been collecting and selling cans and bottles. Send this to the Kurdish mothers," she said in a whisper. She had heard of my efforts to raise money to send to Kurdish refugees heading for the mountains in the aftermath of the Gulf War. "I'm a mother and I know how it feels to lose one's child," she added.

In my new life in the U.S., I learned that the world's poor, whether they lived in the mountains of Kurdistan, the shantytowns of India, or in Portland's housing projects, shared the misfortune of being marginalized, powerless, and voiceless. I realized as long as my forehead was stamped with the word "refugee," I too was a member of this global community. I saw that the world is not divided between the superpowers, the West and the East, or the First World and Third World, but is split between those with power and access to resources and those without. To me, the refugees from Vietnam, Cambodia, Russia, Afghanistan, Iran, Iraq, El Salvador,

Sudan, and Somalia settling in Maine are victims of the cold war and misguided international policies, invasions, and conflicts in the name of national security or profit. We are the road kill of international diplomacy in the race for supremacy by powerful governments.

"Where is home for you, Maine or Iran?" I am asked at times. Though I like to think I belong to every land, as a world citizen of some sort, I feel homesick whenever a soft rain falls, reminding me of the wild tulip-covered hills in spring in Kurdistan with the bright sun peeping like a shy Kurdish girl from behind a white cloud. At other times, when I am away from Maine, I miss its rocky coast and the islands scattered like emerald stones in the blue Atlantic. Years ago, on a trip to Tehran, I woke up the morning I arrived to the sound of *azan* (the Muslim call to prayer) from the neighborhood mosque, the sounds of sparrows in the yard, the smell of familiar spices, and the aroma of Persian tea brewed in a pot sitting on top of a hissing samovar. At once I felt at home.

Salman Rushdie writes, "It may be argued that the past is a country from which we have all emigrated, that its loss is part of our common humanity." I wonder if both past and present could be home—both the taste of the freshly baked naan or my mother's rosewater-scented scarf, and the excitement I feel as my family gets ready for Thanksgiving dinner in Maine, or picking wild blueberries in a field overlooking Frenchman's Bay on a warm July day, or swimming in Sebago Lake.

As I write this, I wonder what remains of the life I left behind. Something tells me the gypsies, who used to cross borders, without official papers, into countries from Europe all the way to India are no longer able to do so. I know Khanum is gone. So is the old house where the gypsy woman came to read Mother's palm. If I were to close my eyes, I could still see the gypsies, my old school whose classrooms smelled of orange blossoms in spring, the green river where I learned to swim, my father sitting cross-legged reading the poetry of Rumi, and the Kurdish musical duo going from door to door to play happy tunes during *Norooz* (New Year), but I know with tender sorrow my memories of the past are fading with time.

Yet sometimes these memories are all we have. In the pages of this book, the memories of twenty-five immigrants to Maine are captured in an attempt to ensure they do not vanish, the way people and cities have done. As Milan Kundera says, "The struggle of man against power is the struggle of memory against forgetting."

In these terrifying days of ours when old men in power dream of invasions, and children in search of food step on land mines left behind by invading armies, and history is being rewritten, it is important to honor each other as members of one family. We may not understand our new neighbors' languages, but for the most part their stories and struggles are the same as ours. Neighborhoods might be built with stones and bricks, but they thrive only if they are based on sisterhood and brotherhood. This book tells our new sisters' and brothers' stories as they make Maine their home.

INTRODUCTION

Maine shows one face to casual tourists and a surprisingly different one to those who look more closely. While it remains one of the whitest states in the country, it looks far less homogeneous than it did just a generation ago. In earlier times, "immigrants" primarily meant French Canadians or Europeans, whose cultural backgrounds were not dramatically different from Mainers'. In the early 1980s, a wider cross-section of humanity, from very different cultures, started arriving.

Who are these new Mainers, and why have they come here? As you will discover in this book, they are from war-torn countries such as Somalia, Sudan, Afghanistan, and Cambodia; from poor Latin American nations; and from economically vibrant places like Hong Kong, India, and Europe—in other words, from across the global spectrum. They came to Maine for a job, or to reunite with their family, or because they fell in love or attended college here, or fled persecution in their homelands. A minority of them are refugees; others hold green cards as permanent residents, or special visas for temporary workers. Some are caught in immigration limbo. While many have become U.S. citizens, others have not, but hold no less allegiance to the state. Quite a few never planned to stay, but did. What they say they found in Maine was a safe, small, family-friendly environment.

Although the twenty-five immigrants who tell their stories in the following pages had widely varying reasons for coming to Maine, many have wound up making remarkable contributions to the state. Some contribute high-level skills in medicine, engineering, academia, law, public school education, hotel management, and social services. Others have enriched the state's arts and sports worlds; for example, as a museum director, a musician, an athletic coach, or a soccer organizer. Several are used to going back and forth across borders, either as transnational professionals or as migrant workers. About one-third of these immigrants are successful entrepreneurs, having started a flooring company, a restaurant, a media company, a catering business, or a refugee-assistance agency.

Several of the immigrants cited education, whether completing high school or earning a college degree in Maine, as the thrilling fulfillment of a dream and the reason for their success in building a good life here. For example, many of the women work in jobs or play dynamic leadership roles in their communities as a result of education they got in Maine and liberal attitudes that allowed them to take on responsibilities they probably couldn't have in the more closed societies from which they came.

One-third of the people profiled here took on new roles as cultural bridges between different ethnic groups, and between immigrants and native-born Mainers. As a social worker, a teen advocate, a job-training consultant, a classroom aide, an immigration lawyer, or a teacher of cross-cultural awareness, they all help immigrants and Mainers get to know and respect each other and resolve conflicts between them.

One of the themes to emerge from the stories in this book is transnationalism. Several of these immigrants found that the immigration experience itself, or global business travel, or migrating back and forth across borders for work has created in them a sense of "one-worldness" or easy comfort in two cultures. In some cases, they have become involved in charity work in their home countries—for example, a refugee who is helping to get a school built in her former Sudanese hometown, an educator/healer who delivers medical supplies when he returns to Nigeria, an engineer who raises funds for a child in China, and a physician couple who provide free services to earthquake victims in Pakistan.

The immigrants' contributions to Maine seem even more remarkable considering the challenges they faced coming here. The refugees' first challenge is to survive economically, while still shadowed by physical and mental health problems caused by the trauma of war or persecution in their homelands. Like them, other immigrants who live here for long periods of time without their spouses, children, and extended families may suffer from loneliness and social isolation. Many of the people in this book expressed that pain feelingly. They may dream of returning to live in their homelands someday, but have to let it go.

Meanwhile, the American dream doesn't always come true for immigrants, or it may take far longer to achieve than they imagined, as can be seen in some of the stories in this book that tell of false starts, disappointment, and family disintegration under the stress of trying to get ahead in a new land. Even after years of living here legally, immigration issues haunt some new Mainers.

Aborted career aspirations are a challenge for many immigrants. Someone with a university degree may find it hard to swallow working in a factory here, and a former nurse may have to work as a dishwasher, because their professional qualifications are not accepted in the U.S. Yet some of the nicer surprises among the stories in the following profiles were the ways in which immigrants had reinvented themselves, finding satisfaction in new vocations. For those who know no English when they come here, communication presents another huge challenge. Some immigrants are working so hard at two jobs that they have no time to take English classes. Their children surge past them in learning the language quickly, creating tensions and power struggles at home.

Most of the immigrants in this book have felt torn between two cultures, missing the language, style, and sense of community they left behind. Some found Americans' emphasis on individualism and the go-go pace of life off-putting and stressful at first. Their sense of loss lingers years after coming here, no matter how well they integrate into life in Maine. But it often leads to new friendships, organizations, and cultural expression, as people from the same countries find each other and rediscover their cultures in a new context.

An ongoing challenge for many new Mainers is bigotry. All of the people of color interviewed for this book have experienced racism to one degree or another in Maine, although they don't believe it is worse here than in the rest of the country. Most of them faced racism here for the first time in their lives, since their skin color wasn't an issue in their own societies. For some, that confrontation caused them to explore the issue with their Maine communities, taking on leadership in civic groups, or the arts, or Maine's schools, where they contribute to our national dialog about race.

One particular challenge, adjusting to life in Maine as a non-Christian, emerged as a theme. Especially after 9/11, some Muslims have come up against hostility in Maine, as elsewhere in America. But for the most part, traditional Mainers have accepted their Muslim neighbors and benefited from learning about Islam—as well as other religions such as Sikhism and Buddhism once rarely found in the state. As many of the people profiled in this book demonstrate, their religion is a powerful sustaining force in their lives as they navigate this new culture.

For many of these immigrants, coming to the U.S. has caused them to examine who they are. A person's self-image as a valued member of society in his or her homeland, or as a fighter for a cause during wartime, or as a person of faith, may undergo a troubling upheaval after arriving in the U.S. Immigrants struggling to fit into the new culture may be scorned as "too American" by their compatriots. One's very identity may be shaken, since where we are from largely defines who we are. As you will find out in the stories that follow, the journeys of these immigrants have not been easy, but all of them are glad they wound up in this state, and are proud of their new identities as Mainers.

NEW MAINERS ✛ *Portraits of Our Immigrant Neighbors*

HOORIA MAJEED

Hooria Majeed fled Kabul twice—first to escape the mujahaddin, and later, the Taliban. She experienced so much heartbreak and fear during the long years of warfare that when she had to leave her homeland forever and come to Maine, she didn't bemoan starting life over.

"I'm worrying before, but happy now. A new life! No bombing, no rockets. A different life," she recalls thinking when she arrived in Portland. Since then, the independence for which Afghans are known seems to have found full blossom in her, as she builds a new career and raises three sons on her own, in a new land.

A decade ago, Hooria lived with her husband and children in Kabul, where she had grown up in an educated, progressive family and worked as a nurse. Her husband, Abdul Karim Majeed, was a well-known artist whose paintings and sculptures graced the homes of art lovers in Afghanistan and beyond. Despite the violence going on around them—first the Soviet–Afghan War, then civil war—the family endured and lived happily. Then one day the Taliban came knocking, pronounced her husband's artworks un-Islamic, and murdered him. Hooria escaped with her children to Pakistan.

Arriving in Portland in 2002 as refugees, Hooria and her sons quickly adapted to America, and she has created a new career for herself as a chef and much-in-demand caterer. A visit to her apartment in Munjoy South, a housing complex on Munjoy Hill in Portland, shows a family focused on the future, with a photo album filled with pictures of Hooria's prized heaping platters of Afghan rice and lamb, eggplant and yogurt, pumpkin ravioli, creamy rice pudding, and other delights.

Her former life is captured in other photo albums, and in the few pieces of her husband's artwork she was able to grab when she left. One framed picture shows two scraps of exquisitely delicate watercolors he painted in his youth—one of a coat and hat hanging on a wall, the other of a man in tribal dress mounted on a horse; their son Sediq hid them in a book before fleeing Kabul. Not much else is left of the works of one of Afghanistan's best artists of the modern era.

Hooria was sixteen years old when she and Abdul Karim married. He was twenty years older, but she didn't object to the marriage, which had been arranged by their parents, who were close friends. Both fathers held high-level positions in the country—her father as a public-works director, and Abdul Karim's as a general in the Afghan army. When her parents asked her if she agreed to the marriage, she replied, "You know what is best for me," although she didn't really understand what was happening, she says. Because they were modern families, there was no "bride price." Male and female wedding guests mingled freely at her parents' home in Darulaman, the western Kabul neighborhood that is home to the onetime royal Darulaman ("abode of peace") Palace, which now lies in ruins. The Soviet–Afghan War was well underway.

Hooria was born during the waning days of the reign of Afghanistan's last king, Mohammad Zahir Shah. She grew up during the 1970s, a turbulent time of political coups and Soviet-backed Communist governments, until the Soviets invaded the country in 1979. She spent most of her childhood in Kabul, except for three years lived in a magically beautiful part of the country when her father took the family with him to Taliqan, a provincial northern town, where he oversaw production at a nearby salt mine. Hooria, who was five when they went, remembers that she and her sister were the only girls in the village school, and children laughed at their city clothes. She found the grand mountains and sparkling rivers in the peaceful region exhilarating.

Hooria's three sisters, two brothers, and she grew up in a modern household and were given loving support by their mother, who stayed home with them. Culturally, the era was liberal, under Communist leaders determined to radically reform the conservative Muslim society and upgrade the status of women. Hooria wore no *chadri*, the full-body covering customary for women in an earlier time and mandated later by the Taliban. She attended school, graduating from Lycee Mariam after her marriage, and finished nursing college.

She and Abdul Karim had three sons—Tarik, Sediq, and Sameer. She worked as a nurse at a Kabul eye hospital, placing her sons in daycare there. As a child, she had been attracted to nursing when she saw women in white uniforms with white hats and noticed disapprovingly that some nurses were not very competent.

"When I'm a nurse, I'll help the sick people," she told herself. At the eye hospital, she was able to do just that, checking blood pressure, giving injections, and prepping patients for surgery. Her husband approved of her working.

Abdul Karim's career was in full swing, with commissions for family portraits and popular interest in his uncannily lifelike sculptures of animals. At least one piece, a sculpture of a horse, was on display in the Kabul Museum, the national museum of Afghanistan, once considered to have one of the most important collections in Central Asia, with objects going back millennia. He painted, drew, sculpted and created masks, besides teaching at an art institute. Through exhibits of his work and the public art he created, he became famous, Hooria says.

His artistic gift had been noticed when he was a student, and the Afghan government had sent him to Germany for three years of college. Later, through his travels in Europe and India, he acquired clients in several countries and facility with seven languages. Although when most people think of Afghan arts, carpets and calligraphy come to mind, in fact, Hooria says, "modern people" had paintings and sculptures in their homes, as her parents did. Her husband made good money from his art, supporting his growing family well and lovingly. "He was a good man," says Hooria, who delighted in his great intelligence and hilarious sense of humor.

After the Soviet forces withdrew from Afghanistan in 1989, the mujahaddin victors fought the Communist-backed Afghan government until 1992, when they captured Kabul. Then the mujahaddin ("holy warriors") battled each other, pushing the country into anarchy and warlordism. As large swaths of Kabul fell into ruins, Hooria and her children became accustomed to seeing men carrying guns and hearing rocket attacks and explosions.

During these tumultuous years, Hooria tried to keep on working at the hospital, but the streets became too dangerous, and life became very hard for women, who had to don the chadri to leave home. The freedom she had known slipped away along with her career. As the fighting kept patients from coming to the hospital, she began doing more and more nursing at her home.

One day, a mujahid came to the eye hospital demanding to see Hooria, but she wasn't there. Knowing that he intended to abduct her, a colleague of hers lied and told him that she had gone to Pakistan. Then the colleague came to her home and warned her that the mujahid was planning to marry her. In the lawless atmosphere of the time, he could do that, since the mujahaddin just took what they wanted, says Hooria.

"You should all go to Pakistan, tonight," her colleague urged her. And so she left, together with her children, her mother, and her sisters, while Abdul Karim remained in Kabul to work. The frightened group of women and children headed for Islamabad, the Pakistani capital, where they had relatives. Without passports, they had to hire drivers to take them through the mountains to avoid the border crossing, changing cars from time to time. For the first time in her life, Hooria wore a chadri, keeping her head down as her mother advised. When she tried walking, she stumbled and fell because she couldn't see well. "It was scary, a lot," she says of the trip.

The group made it to Islamabad and moved from one relative's home to another for the next three months.

When the Taliban prevailed over the other mujahaddin and seized control of Kabul in 1996, at first many Afghans welcomed their success in restoring order. Hearing reports that Kabul was safer now, Hooria and her family returned.

"We went back because we thought it would be okay," she says. Soon, however, she discovered what life under the Taliban would mean for her. She had never been overtly religious ("I'm Muslim in my heart, not for other people," she says) and had never before dressed conservatively or had any restraints put on her social life. Now, suddenly, she couldn't talk to men or work outside her home. If she left the house to go shopping, she was reprimanded. Once, when the Taliban noticed nail polish on her toenails, they beat her feet hard with a stick.

Worse, the Taliban found out about her husband's artworks. They condemned them, along with his profession itself. "That job is for non-Muslims. You're a *kafir* [infidel]!" they shouted. Abdul Karim stood his ground.

"This is my job. This is what I worked for all my life," he replied.

After several threatening visits, the Taliban broke into the house one day and destroyed his artworks—the ones they found, that is. The family had hidden some in the house and buried others in the yard. Soon afterward, the Taliban caught him when he left the house one day, shot him, and dumped his body at the back door, departing with a warning knock on the door. Her sons were at home when Hooria opened the door and started screaming. Later, her arms and legs turned black and blue from beating herself in grief.

There was nothing to do but seek refuge once more with family in Islamabad, where Hooria's siblings already had fled from Taliban-controlled Kabul. She again put on the chadri and left her home, this time forever. Whatever artworks remained at the house were lost when it was later bombed, she heard—a fate similar to that of the irreplaceable antiquities the Taliban smashed at the Kabul Museum and the monumental Buddhas they destroyed in Bamian.

Again, the family group hired a series of cars to take them through high mountain passes to evade border guards. Rockets exploded nearby as they made their way as secretly as they could. In the darkness, no one could turn on a light or someone would warn, "Do you want to get us all killed?" Once, a tire got stuck in the sand, bogging them down. Hooria was terrified.

Finally, they arrived in Islamabad and settled into a precarious life in a city that resented the growing numbers of Afghan refugees.

"The Islamabad police treated us bad," says Hooria, explaining that whenever they left their quarters, the police would recognize them as Afghans and threaten to arrest them if they didn't pay a hefty bribe. Landlords also harassed them, screaming, "Get out of here, you Afghans!" Hooria's world shrank further when her mother died, for she had been a beloved support who shared the raising of her three sons. Once in a while, Hooria visited Peshawar, where her husband's family had fled, and there she obtained Afghan passports for the family.

Stunned by the turn her life had taken, she had no plan for the future. While two of her sisters were accepted as refugees and were sent to California, her own application for refugee status languished. It seemed no one would help her. Finally, after three years, the United Nations responded with a home visit and an interview, and she got approved for resettlement in the U.S.

"I said I'll go anywhere, just out of this place," she recalls. However, as she and her three sons were about to fly out of Pakistan, the September 11 attacks happened, delaying flights for several months. When they finally arrived in Portland, in July 2002, they stepped off the plane into what felt to Hooria's son Sediq like a blast of cold air, since he had become accustomed to Pakistan's sweltering summer. They knew nothing about Maine, and only

Hooria's oldest son, Tarik, knew much English. They were taken aback by American informality, with people saying hi to each other without any of the elaborately formal greetings Afghans exchange.

The three boys, all teenagers, went off to school immediately, leaving Hooria at home and often lonely. Sediq remembers coming home after school some days to find her crying. Hooria's greatest pleasure was in watching her sons do well at school and hearing teachers praise them at parent conferences. Sediq had his own struggle to fit in at Portland High School, but soon found a way.

"The first year, I walked around with my head down. I don't know anybody. The next year, I played football," he says. Not ever having seen the sport before, he saw some boys playing it in Deering Oaks Park one day and thought he might like to try it because it was different from soccer, which his older brother Tarik played. So he sought out a coach, pointed to the football players, and said, "Me play." The coach signed him up, and despite his small size, he turned into a hard hitter for the Bulldogs, making varsity in his junior year and earning a reputation as "the beast from the Middle East."

Hooria, too, found her footing. After a year and a half of studying English, she landed a job as a cook at an Afghan restaurant in Falmouth and honed her culinary skills. When the restaurant closed, she worked for nine months making screen doors at Paradigm Window Solutions in Portland, but had to quit when the work hurt her shoulders and hands. Then, in 2007, the Greek owners of the Acropolis, a Portland restaurant, hired her to wash dishes, and later promoted her to chef. She had learned by observing. As friends sampled her home cooking, word of her talent spread, and soon she was hired for catering jobs—small ones at first, and then larger events.

"My life now is good," she says. She takes pride in her three sons' accomplishments. Tarik is studying computer engineering at the University of Maine at Orono, Sediq is switching from business college to a new goal of attending Southern Maine Community College, and Sameer just graduated from high school. Hooria is planning to become a U.S. citizen. Although she hopes to return to Afghanistan to visit family members who remained, she does not want to live there again.

"Never. After fifty years, maybe it is good," she says ruefully, adding that she hears from relatives about how expensive life is in Kabul, and how difficult the shortage of food, medicine, and other necessities makes living there.

Hooria has other plans for herself, having built a satisfying new life in Portland. She will stay here and put her entrepreneurial spirit to work, understanding that it will take money and patience. "I dream of opening a restaurant—my own business," she says.

JOSE CASTANEDA

"In my lifetime, I have worked the equivalent of two or three people," says Jose Castaneda, and he is still a young man. When he was five years old, he began his work life on the family farm in El Salvador. Since coming to Maine from Central America in 1993, he has taken whatever jobs he could, all of them in seafood processing, with little time for fun. Yet he has carved out one place in his life where he can forget about work and experience pure joy: the soccer field. As founder of a Salvadoran soccer team in 2003, he has helped kick off a soccer craze in southern Maine that brings together players from many different countries who may not speak each other's languages, but share a passion for a sport most Mainers took little interest in until recently.

Jose's wife, Concepcion, remembers when he made the rounds of places with connections to immigrants, like Portland's Reiche School, to drum up support for an adult soccer team, and the idea was laughed at as an impossible dream. But he persisted, as he always has since starting out life as a campesino (peasant farmer) with only himself to rely on.

Born in 1973 in Lagunetas, a small village close to the Honduran border, Jose was one of seven children born to subsistence farmers who grew crops such as corn, beans, tomatoes, and peppers, raised a few animals, and made just enough money to survive. He attended school when he could up to the fifth grade, often leaving early to go to work in the fields. He had to do man's work from a very young age because tragedy had befallen his family: his father had been shot to death in a random robbery attempt when Jose was two years old.

"Only work, work. No time for anything else," says Jose, telling his story in both English and Spanish, with the help of an interpreter. Occasionally, he would kick a soccer ball around with friends.

By the time he was seven, the Salvadoran civil war was underway, turning what was an economically precarious life into a highly dangerous one. The conflict between the government forces, with their right-wing death squads, and leftist guerrilla groups, increasingly targeted peasants, who became the primary victims of terror campaigns during the twelve years of warfare. Jose remembers the fighting, and the devastation left in its wake.

"Helicopters would fly by and shoot, and that would destroy what we had worked on, the animals, too. People would be pointed out and killed. These deaths were not investigated," he says.

When he was a teenager, Jose met Concepcion—or rather, met her again. They had known each other as small children in the village, where her father had a farm, too. But when she was seven years old, her family moved to Citala, a city a few hours from the village, because her father had received death threats. Along with many other campesinos, they sought safety wherever they could to avoid nightly attacks from guerrillas.

"My mother would tell us to sleep under the bed," as the helicopters swept across the area and gunfire shook their house, Concepcion remembers. "Many people would die for any reason." Not taking sides in the conflict, her parents simply waited for time to pass until it was safe for them to return to the village. After the war ended in 1992, they came back. Concepcion and Jose found each other and began to live together. But as life grew more untenable in the village, Jose began to consider doing what his brother and sister had already done: escape to the U.S.

"Since I was small, people would speak about going to the U.S. for a better future. It was something I thought about," he recalls. Concepcion remembers the day he made up his mind to go.

"He put his things together and went. It was difficult for everyone, because nobody knew what would happen. We had heard that many people died trying," she says.

At the age of nineteen, Jose left home and traveled with a group from his village to San Salvador, the capital, where they spent the night getting instructed in how to journey to America, putting themselves in the hands of "coyotes" (smugglers), who demanded half their $3,500 fee up front. Such fees were usually paid by parents, who asked their friends for loans, Jose explains, adding that by now, the price has risen to $10,000.

Traveling on foot and sometimes by car, they made their way north through Guatemala for two weeks, evading the heavy police presence, swimming across rivers, and sleeping on the ground. One of the most frightening parts for Jose was hearing the sounds of wild animals around them. It took another few weeks to cross Mexico, where the biggest threat came from the police, who had a reputation for assault and robbery. Along the way, the coyotes' contacts, and sometimes local citizens, provided what food they could.

"It is difficult to see the other people struggling and starving. If they can find a banana peel, they will eat that," he says. "It is also difficult to trust the coyotes or anyone, because people are trying to take things from you—the little you have. The coyotes don't feel responsible for people who die. If somebody dies, they're just left on the road like a stray animal."

Jose made it across the U.S. border without incident. "I was lucky," he says. From Los Angeles, he flew to Boston on a flight paid for by his brother, and together they worked for a few months on a farm in Massachusetts. In July 1993, Jose moved to Maine to join his sister, who had come to the state earlier.

Meanwhile, back in El Salvador, Concepcion faced a difficult decision. Pregnant with Jose's child and living with her parents, she was urged by her father to follow Jose to the U.S. She would have to leave her home forever to join a group of strangers heading north on a perilous journey. "I was worried. I had never heard of the U.S. I never had it in mind to come," she says, but her father insisted she join Jose because the couple were expecting a baby. He brought her to the city, paid the travel fee, and dropped her off with a single bag of clothes.

"It was a hard decision," she says. "I was scared." Despite being pregnant, she was able to walk days on end through Guatemala, often without food, with a group of about forty people traveling on foot and sleeping on the ground. At one point, somebody warned that immigration authorities were in the area, and she jumped out of a truck onto the ground, badly cutting her knee.

The two weeks spent crossing Mexico presented the worst dangers. Going several days without eating or drinking, Concepcion became so exhausted and dehydrated that she fainted and dropped to the ground, coming close to death. Everyone else in her group was too tired and hungry to help her, and they were about to leave her behind when one old man returned to get her and help until she regained her energy. In Mexico, they swam across rivers at night, afraid of what might be in the water. "It's lucky I knew how to swim," unlike many in her group, she says.

When they finally reached the U.S.–Mexican border it was daylight, so they waited until night to make a dash across a desertlike expanse, breaking into smaller groups to evade detection. Not wanting to be last, Concepcion volunteered for the first group.

"I was very strong. You had to be strong; you couldn't be fearful," says Concepcion, who could hear sirens and see the floodlights of the U.S. Border Control.

Reunited after many months' separation, the young couple started their new life together by working alongside other immigrants on an assembly line in a sea-urchin processing plant in Portland. They received work permits based on asylum from the Salvadoran Civil War. None of the line workers spoke English, so no one complained about the long hours; Jose worked seven days a week, from 5:00 a.m. to midnight, rushing home to sleep for three hours before returning to the plant.

"Your life is just to work," he says of his eight years there. His next job was an improvement—driving a delivery truck for a Portland fish processor for six years. Today, he is employed by another fish processor, Sea Fresh USA, on the Portland Fish Pier, where he works in production and cleans fish and processing equipment. Concepcion eventually moved on to a better factory job. Over the years, they have picked up English by talking to people, but had little time for learning to read and write the language. Besides working full time, they have a busy family life with two daughters, aged fourteen and six, and a son who is twelve.

The Castanedas live the industrious life characteristic of many immigrants bent on getting ahead in America, even though their future is uncertain because of their immigration status. They hold "temporary protected status," which refers to protection from deportation based on ongoing civil strife in El Salvador. Every eighteen months, they pay four hundred dollars to reapply to the U.S. government, which decides whether to continue their status based on whether or not their country's conditions have improved and how well it can absorb numbers of returnees.

"We are still in limbo," says Concepcion, "but we try to have a normal life."

"The most difficult thing is to work hard for fifteen years and not be able to obtain a green card [permanent residency] and visit family in El Salvador," says Jose. They have gotten used to Maine, which they consider a safe, low-key place that is good for raising their children. Over the years, they have bought three different homes and now own two—the Portland one they live in, and another they keep for rental income.

"I am working hard because I want a better future for my children so they don't have to do what I do. If you don't strive to do something for yourself, you're always going to be stuck. You must seek to improve yourself, no matter what your immigration status," Jose says.

His belief in self-betterment extends to his soccer team. Jose takes pride in having built his team up with good players little by little, to the point where they reached their goal as top team.

"Our team is always leading," he says, noting that it consistently wins championships. C. D. El Salvador (Club Deportivo, or Sporting Club, El Salvador) is one of almost twenty soccer teams in southern Maine and is mostly made up of Salvadorans. Although there were few Spanish-speaking players in the Portland area when Jose started recruiting back in 2003, today there are at least four Latino teams.

Their tournaments offer spectators more than the games themselves; they also present bilingual cultural performances highlighting Latin music, food, and pageantry, starting with a blessing of the games by a local Catholic nun. The display may also include a parade of flags; distribution of uniforms to team members by honorary "godmothers," young women arrayed in striking gowns and team sashes; and Latin dance performances. In such measures, tournament after tournament, are native-born Mainers invited to experience Latin American culture.

While no one knows for sure how many Salvadorans live in Maine, Castaneda estimates several thousand. The soccer teams tend to fall into groups from one country or another—Guatemala, Somalia, Sudan, or America, for example—although most teams have a mixture of backgrounds represented.

"Sometimes the players don't understand each other," Jose says, but that's not a problem since "the referee decides what happens, and he doesn't need to speak the languages."

"Soccer keeps people healthy and energized; it's good exercise. And the social part is important," says Jose. "It is becoming more popular. It is fascinating because more children are learning soccer by going to the games and also being coached," he says. Concepcion notes that their own three children aren't especially drawn to soccer, enjoying all different sports instead.

But they know where to find their father on weekends. At least one of the days, he will be on the soccer field. Even in winter, his team plays on—indoors.

"I never stop!" he says.

Khadija Guled

Arrive in Maine after years in a refugee camp, grateful to be alive and welcomed by helping hands. Spend two years in a "honeymoon" period. Then start showing symptoms of trauma, revealing emotional problems buried while dealing with immediate survival issues. As a teenager, struggle to fit in at school. Gain on your parents in English proficiency and exposure to the new culture, causing conflicts at home. Experience frustration in school. Act out.

These patterns are familiar to social workers in the front lines of helping refugees make the hard transition from one life to another. Khadija Guled sees them every day as a case manager at Community Counseling Center in Portland, where a team was set up in 2005 to provide culturally relevant services to refugee and immigrant children with emotional or behavior problems and their families. Her clients include Somalis and other Africans, as well as people from other Muslim countries, such as Afghans. A Sudanese, a Congolese, a Latino, a Cambodian, an American, and an Iranian make up the rest of the multilingual staff at the center.

"It's not an easy job. Everybody has problems," says Guled. "What keeps me going is the resilience these families have, after what they have been through. Some of them have been in the camps for years. It's so scary for them coming here. In spite of all the challenges, they still want a job. They still want to go to school. They still want their kids to do well." Their bravery inspires Guled, who knows how to elicit trust among clients wary of sharing their troubles with strangers.

"People haven't got used to social workers back home, with people coming into their home. If you had a problem there, your counselor was your family," she says. Here, once she establishes trust, her clients become open to receiving help. She works with whatever they need, from accessing services to helping them cope with communication, financial issues, cultural adjustment, mental and physical health troubles, or difficulties at school.

Her clients trust Guled because she speaks their language, and they can relate to her as someone who has walked in their shoes.

As a young girl, Guled dreamed of becoming a doctor, however unlikely that might have been for the daughter of Somali nomads in the Horn of Africa. She was born in 1979 to parents who herded camels, goats, and sheep. Before she was eight years old, she lost both her parents to illness and was taken in by her aunt in the northwestern city of Hargaysa. While her five older siblings went to live with other relatives, she joined her aunt's household, where visits from their large extended family sometimes filled their home with as many as fifteen extra people. From then on, her aunt and uncle became her parents, and their children became her siblings.

She was a keen student at school and sought out science books, especially biology and anatomy. She didn't share her dream of becoming a doctor with her parents, although because they were prosperous, they could have afforded her medical education. "Usually, Somali culture doesn't really nurture talking to children about what they want to be. My parents would have supported it, but people just don't talk about it. Even in Mogadishu, it was normal for girls to get married after high school," she explains.

In the late 1980s, Guled's family moved far south to Mogadishu, where her father had business. But the civil war that had been spreading across the country for four years soon reached the capital, upending her secure life suddenly, in a single day. She had just come home from school and was eating lunch and watching videos with her family, when they heard gunshots. They phoned her father at work to ask what to do, and he said to get a ride to an uncle's home on the outskirts of town, where he would join them. They quickly drove off, carrying only a little food and clothing.

"It was very surreal," Guled says. Today, she recalls certain details of that day, such as the good lunch she was eating and the schoolbooks she brought. "Soon we learned that where my uncle's home is wasn't safe. There was a lot of looting around us. Sleeping was difficult because of the gunshots. We'd go under our beds and hide. That's when I realized that this was the real thing," says Guled, who soon saw the first of many corpses she would see—the body of a man killed by looters in the alley. When her father and other male relatives left for Guled's family home to try to salvage belongings they had left behind, she thought, "I'll never see them again." After a month at her uncle's house, the fighting came closer and got worse, forcing them to flee by car to Kismaanyo, further south on the Indian Ocean.

For a few months, her family lived in a small town near Kismaanyo called Goobwayn. Soon violence caught up with them, killing one of her uncles who was trying to protect them. Her family lived in an abandoned school, eating what little food they had carried and drinking rainwater collected in pots. The men hardly slept at night because they had to stand guard. Guled understood that the murderous attacks going on around her were tribal, clan against clan. "Guns were everywhere," says Guled, whose five-year-old cousin picked one up to play with, and it went off, killing him.

When her own clan was targeted, her family decided to flee further south, toward the safety of Kenya. The night before they left, militiamen swept into the area, killing anyone from her tribe on the spot and massacring those who ran to the beach. Many more families drowned near the beach when the ferryboat to Kenya capsized.

Her family learned of a rough, unpaved passage to the border through the cover of jungle, and "the drivers just went," she says. "We didn't know what to expect there. You just go to escape to safety." Guled's family was lucky to reach the border quickly by car; a lot of others died along the way, or later in the makeshift camp they built in the Kenyan border town of Liboye.

"I witnessed a lot of deaths," from malaria, malnourishment, and murder, says Guled, who had seen too many corpses over these chaotic months. "You fear that you're going to be next. There are people telling you, 'You have to get up, they are coming!'" Guled believes her Muslim faith got her through; it also helped to know that it could have been worse, "because it happened worse to other families." For example, she learned that a mother from her own clan traveling with them had seen her husband and son murdered in front of her.

After some months, aid agencies showed up in Liboye, and for the next several months Guled took turns with relatives standing in lines to receive rations or walking miles to get water. "I remember fighting with kids to get water," she says. To escape the deplorable camp conditions, her family made their way to Nairobi, the Kenyan capital, where they found a house to live in and got used to city lights, cars, running water, and sleeping in beds again. When their refugee status was finally approved after three years, they left Africa for Maine.

Guled was fifteen when she arrived in Portland in the fall of 1994 and picked up her education again at Portland High School. After only one year of ESL (English as a Second Language) classes, she advocated for herself to be mainstreamed because she didn't find the ESL classes challenging enough. She proved herself as a motivated student with good grades. With a strict mother who kept close watch on her despite her own heavy schedule of cleaning offices and caring for the family, Guled stayed focused on her goal of going to college.

Unlike the Somali teenaged clients she sees in her practice today, Guled was able to overcome her childhood traumas without serious repercussions at school; she went on to graduate from the University of Southern Maine's social-work program in 2004. For the leadership role she has since played in Portland, the Maine Women Writers Collection at the University of New England awarded her the Perdita Huston Purple Starfish Award in 2008.

What accounts for her success in the critical high-school years, when so many other students fail?

"I was old enough [when I came]. I had already developed my identity and knew who I was. I struggled with the language, yes, but I had had education and could transfer my math and science skills. A lot of kids arriving from the camps had no education, or their education had been severely disrupted, and they never had the structure of school. It's more difficult for kids in that group, starting here fresh. On top of that, if they're not provided enough extra academic services at school, they never succeed academically," she says.

Guled believes that despite the school system's good intentions, it does not meet the particular needs of immigrants, poor students, and students of color. For that reason, she co-founded an advocacy group, Action for Equal Education, to open a dialog with the schools. "Other states are more advanced. In Portland, they let kids fall through the cracks. We're saying, 'It's time that you pay attention.' If you walk by Portland High School, you see Somali and Sudanese boys hanging around outside," she notes. "A kid I'm working with is a junior, but he has only about six credits. His dad was devastated [to find out] and said, 'I dropped him at school every day.' The kid would just go out the other door"—an example of how students are allowed to drift without sufficient school–parent contact, in her view.

"A lot of kids say, 'Nobody cares about me at school.' I don't think they've been challenged enough," says Guled, who thinks many students stay in ESL classes too long and lose interest, partially accounting for their high dropout rate. Other factors have to do with family. Communication problems develop between parents and their children once the children's English overtakes their parents', causing the parents to feel helpless as the two begin to live in different worlds. The children are experimenting with the new culture while living in subsidized housing where there's a lot of crime and drug dealing, Guled says. Sometimes the parents are working too hard at jobs to keep close tabs on their children.

"Most of the boys have problems in school. A lot have dropped out" after getting suspended for behavior problems and falling behind in school, she says. While the girls take school more seriously, they too are dealing with adjustment issues, fighting at school, and having conflicts with parents—or parent. At least two out of five Somali families are headed by a single mother, either because the father was killed in the civil war or has sent his wife and children to the U.S. without him, says Guled.

"Being a single mom with five to seven kids, trying to be on top of their education and upbringing, they have no time for themselves to pursue education or work. It's a lot of pressure," she says. Many are traumatized by the killing and displacement of war, but bury the emotional symptoms that emerged in the refugee camps for the first few honeymoon years in the U.S. Coming here adds to their stress, and, too soon, financial and other initial settlement support drops away.

"Then suddenly they are on their own. They break down," says Guled. For many, hiding their pain, even though it may be unhealthy, keeps them going. "It has a lot to do with Islamic belief," especially the "Belief in Divine Decree," or fate.

Not all Muslims interpret that belief in exactly the same way. As Guled explains, some Muslims say, "Whatever bad happens to me, I'll accept it; Allah will provide for me." Others say, "You work to help yourself and Allah will help you." But applying a familiar religious lens to unfamiliar American ways of problem solving helps clients cope. Guled cites as an example a meeting she attended with a Somali mother and a probation officer. As the probation officer reassured the mother that he would work with her and things would be okay with her son, the mother answered each of his statements with a prayer: "I pray that Allah will change his heart and raise him to be a good adult."

Educating immigrants and community members like the probation officer about each other's cultures is part of Guled's job. As two findings of the Community Counseling Center's

2006 mental health focus-group session with refugees revealed, overcoming cultural barriers is crucial to effective treatment:

> It was chorused unanimously that mental health providers should respond to their children's and families' needs while understanding they are influenced by their culture and religion, and using families' culture in the treatment process. . . .
>
> Many adult men and women exhibit post-traumatic stress syndrome with severe depression and anxiety. Adapting to a new language and way of life are added sources of stress. Women and seniors feel particularly isolated and lonely.

As a mother herself, Guled can empathize with Somali mothers struggling to raise children caught between two cultures, as she was when she first came to Maine. She also serves as a role model for taking the good from both cultures.

"One of my dreams is to raise my kids with my values, to be good Muslims. I want to travel, to expose them to that, to go back home to meet their grandparents. I want them to have the best of both worlds, so they are well-rounded when they grow up," she says.

"Somalia is my home," says Guled. However, she doubts that she would return to stay. "The country is just ruined by war. I don't know when it will be the time when it will be safe enough for me and my family to live there. I don't think it will go back to the way it was for years to come, but you never know."

Meanwhile, she and her husband, an accountant who works as an auditor for PricewaterhouseCoopers, are comfortable where they are. The two, who knew each other as children and met up again as adults when he moved from California to Maine, like Portland because "it's small enough to raise a family," she says. Their relatives supply childcare for their three young daughters, which will help Guled achieve her dream of earning a master's degree in social work someday.

On a professional and a personal level, Guled projects a calm, steady sense of purpose and ease with herself that comes as something of a surprise, given the horrors she witnessed and the losses she sustained as a child. One wonders how she has been able to come to terms so gracefully with traumas like those for which she now counsels others.

Her answer: "In my life I've been through a lot. One of the things that keeps me positive about life is the rich culture I grew up in as a little kid, and values I learned through the teachings of Islam."

AMARPREET AND HERMEET KOHLI

If it is getting harder for single scholars to find teaching jobs in places of their choosing, or any place at all, imagine the challenge for a married couple like Hermeet and Amarpreet Kohli. Just a few years ago, they were living with their son in Chico, California, where Hermeet was teaching after receiving her doctorate. Amarpreet could only spend weekends with them; the rest of the week he was winding up his own Ph.D. at the University of Louisville, and then was teaching in Kansas. In terms of family life, their next career step wasn't looking much better. Hermeet had been offered a job at San Jose State University in California, and Amarpreet had signed a contract for a position far away, at Northern Illinois University.

"It's very hard to get a job together. I was living with my son in California, and this man was a free bird coming home on weekends," laughs Hermeet, who can smile about it now because there was a happy ending when the University of Southern Maine surprised them with a joint offer. In the fall of 2006, they moved across the country to the Portland campus, where they are both assistant professors, Hermeet in the School of Social Work, and Amarpreet in the School of Business.

"And then God gives us another surprise, a child!" Hermeet says, referring to their second son, born in 2008. Now the family of four lives in a rented house in Cape Elizabeth while they look for a house to buy as they settle further into an unexpected life far from their native New Delhi.

While Hermeet expresses no regrets about coming to America, at one point in her life, she was determined to live in Delhi forever. As the daughter of an Indian Foreign Service diplomat, she had grown up on the move. When she was born in 1973, her mother had come to Delhi from Afghanistan, where her father was serving as ambassador. Thereafter, Hermeet spent her childhood in different countries every three years, with alternating stays in Delhi. She was educated mostly in international schools under the British system, in places as varied as Sudan, Kuwait, Warsaw, and Toronto. Between embassy postings, her mother taught music in Delhi schools, and the family lived a comfortable, upper-middle-class life. While Hermeet found her upbringing stimulating, she discovered one disconcerting drawback.

"The biggest challenge was not being able to live in one place and put down roots." But staying forever in India was not to be. A few years after her marriage to Amarpreet in 1998, her husband decided to get his Ph.D. in the U.S.

Amarpreet, or fate, or both, had indirectly brought the couple together in an arranged marriage. His cousin's brother was seeking a wife, and as a favor, Amarpreet wrote an ad for the matrimonial section of a newspaper on his behalf; the result was a match with Hermeet's cousin's sister. At the time of their wedding, Hermeet's and Amarpreet's families were already aware of each other. As she puts it, in a fashion that may sound endearingly familiar to fans of Bollywood wedding scenes, "My mom's older sister is married into a family in which Amarpreet's father is a nephew of my mom's sister's husband." The many family players had come together, but it all began with Amarpreet's newspaper ad. "That ended up getting us married," says Hermeet, whose mother had often told her, "I have to get you married. I have to get you married!"

The first step toward marriage was discussions between Hermeet's and Amarpreet's parents, followed by a *roka*, or engagement ceremony, where both families met. The couple, who had seen each other often at various gatherings, were allowed to take a walk and talk with each other for a few minutes, after which they told their parents that they agreed to marry. Their parents asked them if they had been subject to any outside pressure, to which they answered no. At that point, they were free to date, and both families exchanged gifts. Nine months later, they married in a hectic five-day whirl of wedding celebrations attended by more than one thousand guests. ("It was tiring for both families," says Amarpreet.)

The Kohlis are Sikhs, but the fact that their marriage was arranged was "more an Indian thing than a Sikh thing," according to Hermeet. The actual wedding ceremony followed Sikh custom in that it took place in the morning and involved reading from the Sikh holy book, followed by a banquet. Both the couples' families are Sikhs whose ancestors were from Punjab, a highly productive agricultural region straddling the border between northern India and eastern Pakistan. While numerous ethnic groups and religions characterize the area after centuries of crisscrossing invasions, today Sikhism is the dominant religion of Indian Punjab.

As British rule in the Indian subcontinent came to a close in 1947, the region was partitioned into East Punjab, which became part of India, and West Punjab, which became part of Pakistan, amid horrific violence in which hundreds of thousands of people are estimated to have lost their lives. Amarpreet's parents, living in neighboring Kashmir at the time, were among those whose lives were turned upside down as children.

"My mom's parents were very rich; they were big landowners" with many servants, he says. "My grandfather was in buying and selling gold jewelry and coins." Suddenly, the new Pakistani authorities ordered all the Hindus and Sikhs to leave or to convert to Islam. "My mom's father committed suicide because he didn't want to." His wife was killed in a bomb blast during the unrest. Amarpreet's aunt also committed suicide because, at fifteen or sixteen, she was too old to be taken by the Indian authorities who swept in to remove young children to India, and she would be in danger if she remained. Since Amarpreet's mother was only nine, the Indian government removed her, and she wound up in Delhi in 1951.

Amarpreet's father's family had lost everything, too, when he came to Delhi from Kota, Pakistan. Having no money to go to school, he started an automotive shop, which ended up supporting the family, while not making them rich.

"He said, 'Whatever I earn, I earn enough to take care of my family.' My dad was a role model for me. I saw him working hard," says Amarpreet, who was born in Delhi in 1971. He sees in his father's self-made success a connection with his Sikhism, a religion stressing enterprise, diligence, and human relationships, as opposed to the much older Hinduism, with its many-layered mythologies.

"My father was never shrewd. He was a very simple man. In India, they think you have to be shrewd and cunning to be successful in business," says Amarpreet. "I thought it wasn't my cup of tea to go into business. I wanted to study, and my father wanted me to study." So, while his older brother helped their father in the shop and his older sister became a homemaker, Amarpreet left home to get his B.S. in mechanical engineering at RV College, Bangalore, and then worked for eight or nine years as an engineer in the automotive field, gaining experience in production and marketing.

By the time Amarpreet got his M.B.A. in 2000 from the All India Management Association, a management development forum in Delhi, his wife already had her M.S.W. from Delhi School of Social Work at Delhi University. Hermeet was teaching at the university, following two years of practicing social work in different organizations, including as project director for Prayas, a Delhi residential home for runaway and orphaned children. She had also worked as a welfare/probation officer at the Delhi Directorate of Social Welfare and as a domestic-violence counselor.

As a girl, Hermeet had wanted to go into a different helping profession, psychiatry. Her older brother was a medical doctor, and she had already been admitted to medical school in Bihar when her parents said, "No, you aren't going to go to Bihar," an eastern Indian state they associated with crime. "They were protective. We had lots of discussions about how hard it is to be a doctor, and they weren't ready to send me out of Delhi," she says. So she switched to the field of child development, earning her B.S. from Lady Irwin College, Delhi University.

Hermeet's professional and family lives were rewarding, and she felt comfortable in Delhi, surrounded by family. The fact that her husband's family was settled in India had been part of her attraction to marrying into it. Then one day, Amarpreet told her he wanted to go to the U.S.

"There are more opportunities here in higher education. In India, the economy is growing phenomenally, but not in academia. In India, the focus is still undergraduate," he says. The upshot was their decision to try graduate school in Louisville, Kentucky, where Hermeet's physician brother had practiced for years. At his urging, she applied to and was accepted into the University of Louisville's Kent School of Social Work and traveled there in

August 2000 to start a doctoral program. She hadn't applied anywhere else.

"It was karma," she says.

By then, the couple had a son, Jaspreet, almost two, who remained with Amarpreet and his family until Hermeet found an apartment and Amarpreet received a fellowship to pursue his Ph.D. at the same university.

"Those were fun days," she says of their graduate school years at the University of Louisville, even though her husband had to work as a management consultant in California part of that time, and only four other Sikh families lived in Louisville (one of them her brother's, and all of them doctors). For religious services, the family traveled to Sikh temples in Indianapolis or Chicago. Along with her studies, Hermeet coordinated community health organizations and health-education centers under a university grant.

Once she finished her doctorate, Hermeet received job offers from all over the U.S., and chose California State University in Chico, which happens to have a large concentration of Sikhs in the area and temples nearby.

"It's important for us and for our children," says Hermeet, who describes her husband and herself as "eclectic" Sikhs in that they celebrate American holidays and do not adhere strictly to all requirements of Sikhism. Formal observance requires baptized Sikhs to wear the Five Ks (*Kakaars*), or articles of faith: uncut hair, a small comb, a metal bracelet, a ceremonial short sword, and a special undergarment. Men wear a distinctive *dastar*, or turban, signifying respect, honor and holiness. Boys wrap their hair in a *patka*, with their hair knotted on top of the head.

The world's fifth largest religion, Sikhism emerged as an offshoot of Hinduism in the fifteenth century. It is a monotheistic religion stressing devotion to God, as opposed to the many deities of Hinduism. As Hermeet explains it, Guru Nanak, the founder of Sikhism, urged that religion "be a way of life, not a set of regulations," and broke with tradition in emphasizing equality of the sexes and rejection of the caste system. Amarpreet believes that the religion's practicality and emphasis on life on earth, rather than an afterlife, helps account for Sikhs' well-earned reputation as successful entrepreneurs.

In Chico, the Kohlis saw a difference between themselves and the local Sikhs, many of whom had come to the area in the early 1900s from Punjab.

"There was a big gap between their thinking and ours. We're more westernized," having grown up in Delhi, Amarpreet says. Such differences intrigue Hermeet, whose current research focuses on immigrant populations. She has written academic papers on Indian women living in the American Northwest, on Indian women's experiences as recent immigrants, and on biracial families with one Indian and one non-Indian parent.

Generally speaking, the Kohlis found Californians more open and welcoming than many of the Mainers they have met so far, who Amarpreet surmises have "a preset mind" because they lack exposure to other cultures. As a case in point, he mentions a neighbor whose visitors' cars routinely blocked the Kohlis' driveway, even after he repeatedly raised the issue with his neighbor. One day, when Amarpreet slightly scratched a car blocking the driveway as he maneuvered to get out, his neighbor yelled at him, "You crazy people. You come here from a different country and you don't know the rules!"

The Kohlis find it odd that they haven't met their next-door neighbors and that "people don't come out" to meet each other, compared to other places they have lived in the U.S. On the other hand, Hermeet says that the friends they have made in Maine are extremely "dedicated and connected" to them. They enjoy their USM students, who they believe take their education seriously, even as many of them juggle jobs and family responsibilities. At the Business School, Amarpreet misses one thing: cultural diversity, which students could learn from.

While the Kohlis are still adjusting to the relative lack of diversity on campus, the Maine climate, and limited opportunities for socializing with other Sikhs, they are happy with their decision to come. They plan to put down roots by buying a home and becoming U.S. citizens. "To be honest, the life here is pretty peaceful," says Amarpreet appreciatively.

"As immigrants here, we're hopeful," says Hermeet. One challenge they foresee is raising their children as Sikhs in a place where few people are familiar with their religion. Their son Jaspreet reports that some children at his elementary school in Cape Elizabeth have teased him about his long hair and *patka*.

"I tell them, 'They are part of my religion, and I'm proud of them,'" he says. Overall, his school experience is very good, and his classmates show him respect, adds Hermeet. As he reflects on the good things about Maine, Jaspreet mentions he likes that the state has "a lot of historic places," citing field trips he has taken to the Victoria Mansion and Tate House in Portland and the state Capitol and museum in Augusta. Since most of his life has been spent in the U.S., and his younger brother was born here, the question arises: Will the children be able to maintain their Sikh identity?

"We really don't know," says Hermeet, but the Kohlis are doing their best. They are teaching Jaspreet *Gurmukhi*, the Punjabi written language of Sikh holy scripture. Also, while the family speaks English as their first language, along with some Hindi and Punjabi, they are sending Jaspreet to Hindi lessons. Having no *gurdwara*, or place of worship, in Maine to gather in with other Sikhs, they keep a holy room in their home for private worship.

"What's important to us as a family is that we instill good values. We have a strong commitment to hard work," says Hermeet. The Kohlis benefit from a lot of support from parents—Hermeet's spend half of each year in the U.S. with their children, and Amarpreet's mother stayed for several months to help with their new baby.

With the couple's strong focus on raising their children well in a region with few Sikhs amid its growing Indian population, the Kohlis are making a go of it as busy academics who have found a foothold at last in the same state.

MAKARA MENG

Makara Meng's grocery store on Washington Avenue in Portland embodies the new upbeat spirit sweeping Munjoy Hill, the gritty home to successive waves of immigrants. Mitpheap Market spreads its warmth from a spacious niche in the old brick industrial relic of the former J. J. Nissen Bakery. Across the street, a Somali halal grocery and restaurant have sprung up by Silly's, a popular eatery. A few doors down is a Salvadoran restaurant. The third world has come to a neighborhood once dominated by a bakery started by a Danish immigrant in the 1890s.

Meng's welcoming store lives up to its name, Mitpheap, which means "friendly" in Khmer, offering an array of goods familiar to Asians, Africans, and Latinos. Customers come to buy hot chili sauce, fifty-pound bags of Golden Elephant jasmine rice, fresh meat and vegetables, Kung-Fu noodle soup, incense, and even damask window curtains. Behind the counter hang men's shirts, a dress, and a bank of phone cards, popular with immigrants for calls to their home countries.

"We have a little bit of everything," Meng laughs. With her gregarious personality, she thrives on meeting customers and claims that running the store is not at all stressful. "I like the people. Everyone who come here have their own identity. I learn a lot about them. That's why I don't have stress."

But there was a time when stress would have seemed like a luxury to Meng, compared to the hell she endured in Cambodia under the Khmer Rouge regime.

Born near Phnom Penh in 1970 to a Cambodian mother and a Chinese father, Meng had a happy early childhood in which her only problem was getting into trouble occasionally because of her strong will. Her mother was a farmer, her father an entrepreneur who moved the family from town to town in search of business opportunities. After her parents worked for a time for a construction company near Phnom Penh, her father landed a job managing a large farm owned by a kindly military doctor in the western town of Kampong Saom, on the Gulf of Thailand. There, Meng, her older brother, parents, and grandmother enjoyed a comfortable life in a large farmhouse and outings to the seaside, where their employer sometimes let them ride in his boat. Her brother went to college, while she started preschool.

"Life was settled. We begin to have a good family life," she says. That life crashed in 1975, when the Khmer Rouge under dictator Pol Pot seized power. At the age of five, Meng was old enough to record memories of the chaos that ensued, but not to understand what was happening. "That New Year, at first it was all exciting; we go to temple," she recalls. "But the third night, the sky was too bright." She felt something was wrong; the adults were acting odd.

"All of them were packing fast and not talking. A neighbor said, 'Be careful. Don't let anyone in.' The dogs were all barking, the geese were making noise. My dad said, 'Take one thing you love the most,' and I grabbed my piggy bank." As they moved out, Meng noticed that he didn't lock the gate. Meng's family joined hundreds of others rushing from their homes and heard that their next-door neighbor had refused to leave; soon she saw the woman's body on the ground. "I screamed, and then my brother carried me."

She heard people warning them. "Behind us they say, 'Keep on walking.' We didn't know who was 'they,' but their word was so powerful that they didn't have to talk; we just obey. I was thirsty and wanted to buy a juice drink, but my dad said, 'Money have no meaning. Our job is to just walk.' I took my piggy bank, smash it on the street, paper money flying every-where. No one stop to pick it up."

After days of walking, they arrived at a forced-labor camp up the coast at Krong Kaoh Kong, where Meng's father and brother were taken away—her brother to Group 1, for young single men, and her father to Group 2, for older males. Her mother was placed in Group 3, for able-bodied females, and she and her grandmother were assigned nearby to Group 4, for those needing assistance. For the next five or six months, she saw her father and brother occa-sionally, but they weren't allowed to talk to each other. After that, the men were moved, and she never saw them again.

Meng spent more than three years in the camp, living in a barracks with hundreds of other children, weeding rice paddies and living on one bowl of watery rice soup each day until eventually starvation reduced her to "a skeleton in rags." Her spirit remained unbroken, even though the guards beat her often and tied her up, causing wounds that festered on her arms. She sometimes slipped out to visit her mother, whom she was forbidden to see. Once, she heard a guard tell his partner, "Let her go. Let the tigers eat her." Such visits were dangerous also for her mother, who was punished for hiding her daughter and was once threatened with suffocation when a guard put a plastic bag over her head until she passed out.

Everyone in the camp was starving. One day, Meng saw her grandmother go to the kitchen and beg for some soup. A guard told her, "You can't come here," and when she replied, "I'm hungry," he knocked her to the ground, killing her. To Meng, her death was a relief, as it ended her grandmother's suffering.

One of Meng's most painful memories is passing her mother on her way to work in the fields and hearing her mother call to her, but being forbidden to answer.

"She told someone to tell me, 'You're still my daughter.'" Meng felt so guilty for ignor-ing her that she believed her mother would not want her if they could ever be reunited. However, one day in 1979, her mother did come for her; Vietnamese soldiers had invaded Cambodia, driving the Khmer Rouge into the mountains. Camp survivors were crying and running in all directions. Meng was nine years old, and her family was down to just her mother and her.

Not recognizing the skeletal girl at first, her mother asked Meng if she was really her daughter. Noticing scars on Meng's arm, her mother inquired if she had been tied up, but Meng said no, pretending that tight elastic on her sleeve had made the marks. "Oh, I'll have to remember not to make your blouses so tight," her mother said.

"To this day, I never told her what happened, and she never told me what happened to her," Meng says. They had both learned the code of silence that settled over survivors of the killing fields.

Starting their journey into a new unknown, life, Meng and her mother joined hundreds of people on a long walk southeast, to the town of Kampot, near the Vietnamese border, from which they traveled by bus to Phnom Penh, then to Battambang in the northwest. They finished their trek northward on foot, walking at night to elude roving patrols and passing corpses along the way. At last they arrived at a United Nations refugee camp in Thailand, where they lived for three and a half years.

"Everything there was like heaven—school, daycare, food, and I could be with my mom," Meng remembers. There was even money. Her mother, who couldn't read or write, sold gold she had managed to keep hidden in the seams of her clothes during the Khmer Rouge years. Once accepted as refugees bound for America, they were sent to a transit camp in the Philippines, and, after a year, flown to Boston, where they arrived one frigid, snowy day in January 1984 wearing flip-flops. Meng had dreamed of having a nice house in the U.S. Instead, they moved into a cramped house shared by fourteen people in the grimy Allston section of Boston, where Meng got her first schooling. They soon moved again, to a Cambodian community in Lowell.

In time, Meng adapted to America, growing into an independent young woman. That freedom ended, though, when she was twenty-four years old—an "old maid" by Cambodian standards—and her mother arranged her marriage to the son of a friend in their former Cambodian village. Because Meng was by now an American citizen who could bring her husband to the U.S., she agreed to the arrangement as a favor to her mother and went to Cambodia for the wedding.

"I asked my mom, 'Is this a real marriage?' My mom said yes, adding, 'Love can grow.'" Meng realized she had made a big mistake, but decided to give the marriage a chance. In Lowell, she ran a successful home sewing business employing thirty workers, but it was a high-stress time, as she found her husband unsupportive and reliant on her for everything.

With the birth of their two sons, Meng's responsibilities grew. On the advice of a friend, the family moved to Florida for a time to try vegetable farming, but wound up losing money. In 2001, when a relative living in Maine told them about opportunities in the Portland area, Meng's family moved there. Her husband worked at Barber Foods' chicken processing plant, and she worked at JC Penney. "Maine was fine," she says. But her marriage was not; she divorced her husband the next year, and acquired a new stressor: both their sons were diagnosed with autism, and Meng was spending hours seeing doctors and tracking down services, on top of working and running the house.

As her frustrations mounted, so did nightmares and flashbacks of her early life, which she had kept hidden behind a smiling face. Pouring her energies into studies at Southern Maine Community College, she prepared for a career in nursing. One day, she mentioned her nightmares to a classmate, who suggested she see the campus counselor. In sessions with him over the next months, she talked for the first time about the brutalities she had endured at the hands of the Khmer Rouge. Later, she told her story to a Portland newspaper reporter, publicly breaking the code of silence maintained by many Cambodians in Maine.

Meng's openness has earned her a reputation as a "big mouth" among some Cambodian immigrants, who she says take the view that "that's the past; we're here now." To Meng, however, her story is important for her children and others to know. Recounting what she has hidden for three decades brings tears to her eyes, but suffuses her with a grateful perspective on her life. "I'm the most luckiest person," she says.

Others might say she is the most persevering. When Meng bought the grocery from its previous Cambodian owners in June 2007, she took on a twelve-hour-a-day, seven-day-a-week job. With support from family members who work there and help care for her children, she has made a success of the enterprise she dived into on nothing but intuition and a few loans. The customers, her new friends, keep coming.

"I like Maine people. They always have a minute to ask you something and acknowledge who you are," she says.

Meng has remarried—her husband works at Barber Foods and helps out at the store—and they have a young son, who often amuses himself behind the counter while Meng rings up sales and chats with customers. She has dreams for her children. In the case of her autistic older sons, she believes that their uniqueness is a strength: one could be a storyteller because of his strong imagination, and the other, who draws well, could become an artist. As for the youngest, "He bonds us all."

Living in South Portland near the ocean, with her mother as part of her household, echoes the happiest years of Meng's childhood. In fact, when she moved to Maine, her whole life changed for the better, she says. It is a life she has built out of sheer determination and an openness to taking the best from both her cultures—the Cambodian one for which she feels a deep love, and the American one, which gave her freedom and education. Asked what she believes is her main identity, Cambodian or American, she pauses to think for a long moment, and then replies, "I'm a human being."

"Music has no boundaries," says Shamou, who has crossed quite a few geographical ones since leaving his native Iran as a teenager determined to become a musician in America. Having performed from coast to coast, in venues from schools to Las Vegas casinos, he finally settled in Maine, his base for musical connections reaching around the world.

A multi-instrumentalist, dancer, singer, and composer steeped in Eastern, Western, and African diaspora traditions, Shamou arrived on the world music scene at a propitious time, when its popularity was taking off. A believer in life as a cyclical process—his band is called Loopin'—he looks back on certain powerful turning points in his personal and musical journey that propelled him both forward, to deeper understandings and greater accomplishment, and backward, to early influences.

Born in 1960 in Tehran, Shamou (his stage name) came under the spell of American music as a young child, spending hours listening to favorites like James Brown. "The West was a prominent presence and very much admired in the circles I was in," he says.

With the Shah, Mohammad Reza Pahlavi, on the throne, Western culture pervaded Tehran; tapes and vinyl records of American and English pop stars were widely available. Elvis, the Beatles, Santana, Jimi Hendrix, and Pink Floyd were hugely popular. So were Bollywood movies, which Shamou loved and which may partly account for his crowd-pleasing showmanship on stage.

His father, a banker, exposed him to Persian classical music. The affluent household was expansive, busy with family get-togethers, and progressive in its atmosphere. His mother encouraged her six children to explore music and dance, hiring private teachers for them.

"I've been very fortunate," Shamou says, recalling his parents' generosity and the open society under the Shah that offered avenues for growth. As children, his brother and he would grimace when their father played his Persian music. Still, it was an education that would inform his own music one day, playing instruments like the *zarb* (Persian hand drum), the *santur* (Persian hammered dulcimer), and *darbouka* (Arab and Turkish hand drum), and incorporating sounds from Iran's musical crosscurrents—Arabic in southern Iran, Afghan and Pakistani in eastern Iran, and Turkish in northwestern Iran.

"There was such a mixture of different sources of music. Persians for hundreds of years have been fascinated by music, art, and poetry; it was a prominent part of my upbringing," says Shamou, whose father loved to listen to the classical poetry of Hafez, Rumi, or

Khayyam recited while music was playing, the two "bouncing back and forth like jazz." Other family members were musical, too. His older sister played the accordion and won a national music competition in high school.

"I admired her. My brother and I had hand drums. Whenever we had family gatherings, my sister would be encouraged to play, and we would accompany her," he says. Another sister founded a choir and married a musician from the orchestra at the city's opera house, where ballets such as *Nutcracker* and *Swan Lake* were staples.

In fact, Shamou started his performance career as a ballet dancer, following in somewhat different footsteps from his older brother, who danced with a troupe for TV shows. When Shamou expressed an interest in ballet at the age of ten, his mother hired a principal dancer from the Iranian National Ballet to prep him at home for entry to the dance school that trained young corps de ballet dancers. He danced with the ballet company for several years, including some performances in front of the Shah and other dignitaries.

"I had a great time. I realized I wanted to be a performer," he says, recalling the thrill of stepping onto the stage with his heart pounding. A highlight was dancing in a production of a story from the *Shahnameh (Book of Kings)*, Ferdowsi's epic Persian poem, a performance the Shah particularly loved.

"Then I grew tall and went back to music," says Shamou, who stands six feet seven inches today. By the time he was sixteen, he knew he wanted to go to America and be a musician. His parents agreed to a first step: going to England to study, under the guardianship of family friends living there. So Shamou left his home for London and a boarding school in Wales, where he perfected the textbook English he had learned in Tehran. While there, the 1979 Iranian Revolution overthrowing the Shah, the U.S. hostage crisis, and the 1980 siege of the Iranian Embassy in London exploded in images in the British news media.

"Those images were as shocking and disturbing to me as the images of the Twin Towers" of the 9/11 attacks, he says. "It was like a bad nightmare." Everybody, including some in his own family, lost someone and/or everything they owned, he says. At the time, Shamou's parents were visiting London, but they eventually returned to Iran. He stayed on, studying classical piano for several years with an instructor from the Royal College of Music and playing drums informally.

Eventually, he got his wish and came to America at the invitation of a friend. Compared to England, with its politeness and old culture, America seemed wide open, and, after a bout of culture shock in Manhattan, he set out to explore it.

"When I came to America, I started going on a quest—a period of self-discovery and education. I was learning a lot about the way of the world, the way of the West, the open spaces," says Shamou, whose nomadic journey took him across the country to San Francisco. During a stay of several years at a ranch in New Mexico, he found a spiritual home for a time in a setting that reminded him of childhood family trips to the mountains in Iran.

"I had an education about life, living sparingly with nature, gathering wood, raising livestock, making goat cheese," he says. One day, when a doctor in the community loaned him his conga drums, Shamou rediscovered his love of drumming and bought a drum set. "I would play the stereo and sit behind the drum set for hours."

Deciding he needed to get on a more organized track, he enrolled in San Juan College, a community college in Farmington, New Mexico. Even though he was studying industrial electrical engineering ("Persians are notorious for their engineer and doctor degrees, encouraged by their parents," he says), Shamou spent all his free time playing drums in various ensembles. The college's music director, Rich Levan, was a drum player himself.

"He became the sage and guide that I needed at the time," says Shamou, who also learned from Indians he got to know from attending their sun dances and rain dances where he was living, in the Four Corners region that is home to Navajos and Utes.

"I consider my years in New Mexico a tremendously significant part of my life. I learned a lot about the West, connecting with the Native Americans there, and experiencing that vast space," he says. After this turning point, he was ready to dive into professional musical training. On Levan's recommendation, in 1989 Shamou entered the Berklee College of Music in Boston, a city he fell in love with immediately for its European-style architecture.

He calls his years there "tremendously fruitful, educational, and multidimensional," coinciding as they did with an explosion in world music and jazz. He made a name for himself as a multitalented drummer, and became the lead singer and percussionist with award-winning world-music ensembles. Persian music caught up with him when he accompanied Persian pop stars he had listened to growing up. He also began collaborating with dancers, working with greats such as the Alvin Ailey American Dance Theater.

Shamou's last year in Boston marked yet another turning point in his life. "I had been developing themes, sketches, and compositions for several years. It was time to give form to them by completing my first self-produced solo CD, *Spirits Dance*," he says. Its release at the end of 1996 put an official seal on his musical journey and was a personal marker, as well, since during the year-long process of creating the recording, his father passed away. To Shamou, symbolizes a right of passage, a key that continues to open doors.

In 1997, Shamou got a call from Laura Faure, director of the Bates Dance Festival, a nationally recognized contemporary dance festival at Bates College in Lewiston, Maine, inviting him to participate in the event. He played music there that year and the next, although he had moved back to San Francisco to work with a dance company and finish a CD with his band at the time, Shodjah.

When the group subsequently disbanded, Shamou went out on his own. From 1998 to 2001, he played solo drums to electronic music with DJs in venues drawing thousands of fans, such as San Francisco's Fillmore West, Great American Music Hall and Bill Graham Auditorium, along with other clubs and casinos on the West Coast and in Las Vegas.

"I was riding a high because what I was doing became popular. I was performing, putting on a show," sometimes, in costume, hamming it up, he says.

Eventually, he became disenchanted with the big club scene and Las Vegas, where he played regularly and watched bands in their later years performing as if they were in a time capsule. "It's either that, or you evolve," he thought. He was ready to move on when the September 11 attacks struck, grounding air traffic, crippling the entertainment business, and bringing Shamou to another turning point.

"I decided to leave that life behind after 9/11. I thought, 'I've had my ride.' I had a lot of recognition in that scene," he says. "I wanted to come back to composition. I was playing like a maniac, and my creative juices had stopped flowing."

Meanwhile, he and Laura Faure had stayed in contact, and he wound up joining her in Maine in 2002; they were married the next year. While love drew him to Portland, he was pleased to discover there was a lot going on musically in the city.

"When I decided to come here, people came out of the woodwork," he says. One was a musician he had met in Berkeley, California, while on tour with a percussion ensemble. They formed a world ensemble, Loopin', which combines Middle-Eastern, jazz, Afro-Caribbean, and American mountain music with an electronic dance beat. With his compositional juices flowing once again, he has since created a second self-produced solo CD, *Traces*, in addition to releasing two group albums, and he has enough material for five or six more CDs in the studio of his Portland home. He also spends a lot of time traveling and doing presentations and residencies in schools and colleges.

"It has turned out to be quite a calling doing residencies in schools across the state," says Shamou, who has taught hand drumming, percussion, and music for dance across the country since 1990. To him, teaching is enriching both for those who receive it and those who give it. "You either hold onto knowledge and put a moat around it, or you share it," he says. He continues to perform, dazzling audiences with his versatility in various drumming traditions and making new musical connections from Maine to places as far away as Mexico and Senegal.

Cycling back to childhood influences, he introduces classical Persian elements into his music. He has found several opportunities in New England for expressing those influences—for example, creating music for a cultural exploration of the Shahnameh as part of the Arts Alliance of New Hampshire. He composed music for and performed in Portland Stage Company's *Yemaya's Belly*, and has danced with the Portland Ballet.

Shamou has composed original scores for works by the Sacramento Ballet, Prometheus Dance Company, and other dance groups, as well as for several well-known choreographers during residencies at the Bates Dance Festival.

Lately, Shamou, who is a U.S. citizen, has started to feel the pull of visiting his homeland, which he has not seen since he left as a teenager.

"I see myself going back as an elder, seeing places I never went to, and reconnecting with the past. I'm interested in the roots of Persian history; it is one of the main things calling to me, and also the music. There are so many incredible Persian musicians here and in Europe and Iran, so impressive and virtuosic," says Shamou. And while Western music may be frowned upon in Iran today, Iranians are still listening to it, says Shamou, adding, "You don't need a passport to listen to music from another part of the world."

Going back would complete one of the circles in his life—the connection to ancient Persia he feels that causes him to identify as a "Persian," rather than an Iranian. He does not pine over the loss of his culture as some immigrants do, perhaps because he has stayed connected to it through music. How one deals with loss depends on one's perspective, he says, offering a metaphor:

"What is it we're losing? Drummers 'shed'—when you're practicing, the sticks shed, and eventually break. But by going through that process, you master your instrument and become more accomplished. We shed our skin, too, but we're still intact and we have grown. Yes, it's a loss. How much weight is given to that loss determines how far it pulls you back or how far it can pull you forward; the cycle keeps repeating. Music is an incredibly important part of it. It's a unifying force wherever you go in the world."

MARY OTTO

"Girls never go to school," Mary Otto's uncle scolded her after she followed her male cousin to school one day and stubbornly sat outside the building for the entire day after the teacher told her to go home. At the age of five, she was already working as a babysitter for her uncle, who reminded her that girls should get married and take care of their families, period. "That was the end of it," she says.

Or so she thought at the time. In May 2008, Otto graduated from the University of Southern Maine with an associate's degree, at the age of fifty-four. During the intervening years, she did what she was supposed to as an Acholi woman of Southern Sudan—raised a family—and much more, besides. With quiet perseverance and the encouragement of a beloved father, she eventually got schooling and worked at jobs outside the home. Then, in the 1990s, Sudan's civil war forced her to call on a different kind of intelligence that she possessed in great quantity: the quick-witted resourcefulness needed to live on the run from bullets.

Much of Otto's life has been spent on the move, starting with her parents' departure from Agoro in Southern Sudan, where she was born in 1956, the year Sudan won its independence from British/Egyptian rule. Her father was angry over family pressure for his widowed mother to marry her brother-in-law, according to tribal custom, so he took his family to neighboring Uganda, where they lived for five years with his brother's family.

When her parents moved on to Nairobi, Kenya, with her older brother and baby sister, they left five-year-old Mary behind to care for her baby cousin. She didn't see them again for four years. "In my culture, they want you to help your family members," and it is more common for girls to care for relatives' children than for their own younger siblings, She explains. Otto was happy in the household, among family who loved her.

When her father found out that Otto wasn't attending school, he was upset. He brought her to his home in Nairobi, where his younger brother and he held telecommunications jobs at the city's airport. He enrolled her in a Roman Catholic orphanage school, where, with his help, she learned the ABCs of Acholi, their native language, and studied Swahili and English. While her father knew how to read and write, her mother was uneducated.

"She had ten children. She was just cleaning, cooking, every day. That was her job. I felt so bad for her," says Otto, who knew she herself wanted more.

"I loved school so much," she says. "It broke my heart when my father couldn't pay my school fees any more. I saw him going through pain. I loved him so much, so in seventh grade, I dropped out. I said, 'Just pay for the boys. My brothers need to be educated.'"

Once again, Otto's family moved away and left her behind. Her father's mother had called him back to Sudan to help the family, and as the eldest son, he had to obey. She took care of the many children of her uncle, who had three wives living together in the household. Observing the struggles of the large, somewhat unstable family, she formed the view that having so many children, not because they really wanted them, was the cause of their hardships.

Meanwhile, she became close to the Catholic Church. Content with her life, Otto gave little thought to marriage.

"I looked at the boys like my brothers. I'd say to them, 'We are friends.' I was so quiet. People teased me: 'You're not ever going to have a baby.'" Instead, she trained as a typist at Garden Secretarial College in Nairobi. "English was so hard, but I stick in there and graduated!" she says.

In 1978, Otto's father died, leaving her bereft. "Who am I going to now? My father's dead. Why should I not be by their side?" she asked herself. So she rejoined her family, now living in Kit, in Southern Sudan. She got a typing job at a community-development office in Juba, the regional capital of Southern Sudan, and soon began to change her mind about marriage.

"My culture respects married women. I thought, 'Maybe I'll get a man who is like my dad, someone I can look up to.' That was not what God wanted," says Otto, who at twenty-seven married a senior community-development officer with whom she worked, and they moved to Yambio, in southwestern Sudan. Things went well at first, and a son was born, but the marriage soured when her husband began beating her. He also took up with other women—a situation she accepted out of concern that she would never remarry if she left him, and fear that one of his girlfriends would harm her.

Otto had promised God that she would have four or five children, if she could. She kept her promise, with the births of another son and three daughters over the next several years. At the same time, she continued to work as a typist. She kept the family together and carried on, until rumblings of war to the east began to reach her area.

By 1983, civil war had broken out, pitting the Muslim Arab northern forces of the Islamic central government against rebels from the predominantly Christian, non-Arab south. Otto's region remained quiet until one day in 1991, when the rebels arrived five days after she had given birth to a daughter.

"People started running. My husband said, 'We'll go to the rural area and hide.' The people left. We can hear the guns, the bombs," Otto recalls. Government soldiers approached her with the warning, "Get your children and leave." That evening, the family camped next to a lake, the children hidden behind a tall anthill. When shots rang out in their direction, they all fled.

"I carried the baby in my arms, and belongings on my head," says Otto, whose husband and brother-in-law mustered the other children as they all ran to the forest. "More bullets were pouring. We were in the hand of God. Until today, I think, 'How did we survive?'" In the forest, where it was cold at night, the new baby became sick and couldn't nurse. Otto was determined to take her to a nearby hospital, but as she set out, she heard the pounding sound of rebel soldiers' marching feet.

"Let's shoot them," some said when they spotted villagers. "No, they're civilians, with babies," said others. Otto had heard that some of the rebels "did bad things," yet she continued on toward the hospital they occupied.

"I was talking to the rebels. I said, 'You're fighting because of us,'" says Otto, whose friendly words were rewarded with gifts of blankets and medicine.

"They said, 'Stay in the bush. Planes are coming [to drop bombs].'" With the situation worsening, her family remained in the bush for the next two months, occasionally sneaking into town for food. On one of their forays, the planes swept across the sky, and she ran for cover behind a sweetpotato hill near a water pump. Bombs fell, killing three children at the pump before her eyes. As more bombs fell, she and her family huddled in the bush until they could join other villagers moving into abandoned homes in town. There they remained for the next nine months until rebels rescued them and took them to Torit, a southeastern city under rebel control.

At that point, Otto began looking for her mother, whom she hadn't seen in years. She found her living with relatives in a grass hut they had built in the bush; they too had moved from place to place. Upon Otto's return, they demanded that her husband pay a dowry of seven cows and ££10,000. "They thought he had disfigured me from beatings," says Otto, pointing to her face; but there was no way her husband could pay. She wound up joining him in Juba, where government troops controlling the city accused him of being a rebel and arrested and tortured him. Rescued by his brother, he took their oldest son and disappeared.

"We didn't know where he was. They started looking for him," says Otto, who was also arrested and beaten, then put under house arrest. One day, she managed to escape with the four children she had with her, and reached her mother, living in the bush in Agoro, Otto's birthplace. By now, Otto had traversed the southernmost states of Sudan, Africa's largest country, five times.

"Those days, you can't tell who is who. Rebels, civilians—everyone had guns. People were doing bad things," she says. To feed her children, she turned to a nearby resource, a river. "I took gold from a river and sold it for food. I had nobody. I had to take care of my children." One day when she returned from panning for gold, she learned that fighting had closed in on where her family was living, and her cousin's wife had been murdered.

"That made me sick. I decided to leave," says Otto, who still didn't know where her husband and oldest son were. "My mom said, 'Don't go. There are bad people everywhere.' I said, 'No. I'm not going to die here.'" With that, she gathered up her children and joined a crowd of others fleeing the area.

"We walked for a month through the bush to Uganda," says Otto. When they reached Nimule, a border town on the Anyama River, Ugandan soldiers stopped them. "Where are you going?" they demanded. Otto could see a large market across the river, so she replied, "I'm going to the market." When they asked, "Then why are you bringing all those children?" she thought fast and answered, "I have to fit them with clothes."

Otto urgently needed to cross the border and get help for her baby, who was desperately ill with yellow fever. But when the soldiers discovered she had medicine, they accused her of being a witch, coming to poison Ugandans. To prove them wrong, she quickly swallowed some of the medicine, which made her vomit. Her other children went on ahead to the market with the crowd, but the soldiers continued to interrogate Otto, who kept her wits about her. Remembering her childhood stay in Uganda, she cried, "I am one of you! I'm bringing my children back to Uganda." When she named the town she had once lived in, the soldiers let her pass.

"Welcome home, sister!" they beamed.

"Sometimes you have to lie to survive," says Otto.

In the market, Otto sold some gold she had hidden on her baby daughter to get the family to the Kiryandongo Refugee Camp in Uganda, where they stayed two months in a sea of misery.

"So many people, sickness, diarrhea, malnutrition, all bloated stomachs, no food," recalls Otto, who labored in local farmers' fields to get a few mangoes for her children each day. From there, they were transferred to the Ifo Refugee Camp in northeast Kenya. Amid terrible conditions, she tried to stay productive, making beer and grinding maize until her hands were blistered. After almost two years, they were brought to another Kenyan camp for processing to come to America. Hearing from other refugees that Portland was a good place to raise children, she was happy to be sent to Maine.

Eight years later, in 1999, Otto was reunited with her oldest son, who had become separated from his father in the fighting around Juba when their car was bombed. "He was eighteen when he came. I left him when he was ten," she says.

Otto's new start in life was not easy, although she liked Portland right away. The English she had once learned had disappeared during her work years, when she typed in Arabic. However, at Portland Adult Education, she quickly progressed from English classes to getting her GED. Then, as she was finishing an office-work certification course, she was offered a job at Portland High School as a language facilitator, helping students in the classroom.

"I came to love my job, and I started sharing my story [with the kids]. Some of these young adults are old already and getting violent," she says, referring to some of the teenaged refugee students. "I said, 'Stop fighting.'" Understanding that they were struggling to overcome the traumas they had experienced and trying to adjust to a new culture, she told them, "If I can do it at forty, you can do it!"

"They really listened to me. They called me 'mom.' They started cooling down," says Otto. Much as she enjoyed her job, however, she had to switch to a higher-paying office job at Blue Cross Blue Shield of Maine for a year and a half when her brother in Khartoum got into an accident and needed money. Discovering that "computers are not for me; I like working with children," she returned to the classroom, this time at Reiche Elementary School, where most of the pupils are from other countries. The job calls on her knowledge of five foreign languages, including Swahili, Arabic, Acholi, Nuer, and Kikuyu.

While Otto is happy in her life, she is conscious of what she has lost in coming to America. "Here, I have so many friends, but still I miss my own family. I grew up in a culture where we value each other and live together. Here, everybody has their own problems. They don't have time to share. My children are in between cultures," says Otto, who speaks Acholi at home to transmit at least some of her culture.

One place Otto finds a close community is in her church, the Cathedral of the Immaculate Conception, where she serves on the parish council. For someone who wanted to become a nun as a child, the church continues to supply deep meaning in her life, as can be seen in the framed religious pictures adorning her living-room walls, alongside the many family photos. As a leader in both the church and in an organization of Maine Sudanese called ASERELA (Action for Self-Reliance Association), Otto has helped raise money for a school in the Kiryandongo Refugee Camp in Uganda. She is delighted that, with life calmer now in Southern Sudan, a new school will be built for refugees returning to the community of Kit, where Otto once lived. "My own backyard!" she says.

Helping children has been a constant theme in Otto's life, since her earliest babysitting days. At home, she cares for two grandchildren after work. Three of her children also share her apartment—her high-school-aged daughter, Rebecca, her daughter Sarah, who attends USM, and her younger son, Joseph. Her older son, Godwin, is in Vermont, and another daughter, Suzy, attends college in Massachusetts. She financially supports her mother, now in Kampala, Uganda, as well as the families of her two brothers, who died after she left Sudan.

"I have so many responsibilities," she sighs, and for that reason she cannot yet take the next step she would like to take: study to become a social worker. Still, having earned her USM degree, she is proud to have come this far on a journey she never thought she would be able to make.

"My dream for school did not fade away," she says.

GERARD KILADJIAN

In the Damascus of Gerard Kiladjian's youth, non-Muslims like his Armenian Christian family lived well. People of both faiths mingled easily and were matter-of-fact about religion. On Friday, his Muslim friends went to the mosque, or not; on Sunday, he and his Christian friends attended church, or not.

"For Armenians living in Syria, it was a very good life. We never felt any difference," he says. "People should look at Syria to learn how Christians lived very successfully with Muslims for many years. There's a way to blend the cultures." In fact, he finds similarities in Armenians' and Arabs' cultural values in the Middle East.

Kiladjian could have remained in Damascus forever, enjoying the best of both worlds. Known as "the Pearl of the East," the fabled Syrian capital is a UNESCO World Heritage Site and one of the oldest continuously inhabited cities in the world. But he couldn't have enjoyed the wide-ranging career he has had in hotel management.

By immigrating to North America, Kiladjian was able to work his way up through a series of hotels in the U.S. and Canada to become the general manager of the upscale Portland Harbor Hotel, Portland's only AAA four-diamond hotel. Happily for his family, he also found the right place to put down roots after years of moves. A well-traveled cosmopolitan who speaks four languages (Armenian, Arabic, French, and English) and combines gregariousness with elegant taste and attention to detail, Kiladjian is well suited to his profession. However, it is his core identity as an Armenian that drives many of his other activities and contributes to Mainers' multicultural awareness.

Although Kiladjian has lobbied for official U.S. recognition of the 1915 Armenian genocide, in which the Ottoman Turks killed at least 1.5 million people, the genocide did not affect his own ancestors. His great-grandparents left Armenia even before earlier massacres, in 1894–96. His great-grandfather on his mother's side was in the horse-trade business, traveling to Syria from Armenia on a regular basis selling Arabian horses. He met his wife, who was an Armenian from Egypt, during one of his business trips, and decided to settle in Syria. Both of Kiladjian's grandfathers worked as doctors in Syria, where his own parents grew up.

Kiladjian's father chose the army for his career. A war hero who was wounded in the 1948 Arab–Israeli War, he quickly rose through the ranks, becoming a widely respected general at the age of thirty-seven. His black-and-white photograph displayed in the living room of Kiladjian's Portland home shows a more serious-faced version of Kiladjian himself, in a uniform bedecked with medals. By the time Kiladjian was born in 1965, his father had been forced to retire following the short-lived union of Syria and Egypt in the United Arab Republic, when the new regime ousted "outsiders" such as Christians from the army. Although his father managed a construction company building grain silos from then on, he never entirely lost his military ways at home.

"We were very disciplined in the house," says Kiladjian. "God forbid I should leave my room if everything wasn't in order." The family's friends always knew when to expect their arrival, because he kept the family precisely on time. His mother, although college-educated in France, stayed home and raised his older brother and sister and him. Their large flat in a five-story apartment building was often filled with friends, and his parents were active in the Armenian community.

"There was always music and dancing in the house when my parents' friends got together. People were always playing the piano and accordion," he remembers. "We wanted to keep the cultural values as Armenians." He spoke Armenian with his mother and Arabic with his father, whose Armenian was weaker.

Syria's middle class included many Christians, who were cultivated by the ruling Baath party's Alawites, themselves a minority religious sect. The Kiladjians lived in an affluent section of Damascus, across the street from President Hafiz al-Assad, whose home wasn't particularly extravagant, according to Kiladjian. Because his father thought he would have a better future if he became fluent in Arabic, he was sent to a school where classes were taught in the language, rather than to an Armenian school, and he studied alongside children of influential families.

"I was a classmate of Bashar al-Assad [the current president] all throughout middle and high school. They were a good family. Bashar was a very honest, straightforward kid. He was well-disciplined," Kiladjian recalls. Bashar assumed the presidency on the death of his father in 2000, although his older brother would have succeeded to the post if he had not died in a car crash; having known both brothers, Kiladjian believes Bashar was the better choice. "His brother would have been tougher politically versus Bashar, who is more easygoing and open-minded, I believe."

In the densely populated city of hot, dry summers and cool, wet winters, people lived in high-rises with cement-block exteriors and cool marble or granite floors with oriental area rugs for decoration. French influence left over from the 1923–43 French Mandate lingered; many people, like Kiladjian's parents, spoke fluent French, and Western dress was the norm.

"When I was growing up, only about 30 percent of women covered [with hejab]," he says, adding that in the last five to ten years, more Muslims are turning toward religion and more women are covering. Classes at his school were coed, with girls and boys alike wearing military-style khaki uniforms. Nationalistic-tinged history classes taught about the Baath party and the Middle East, and nothing about the U.S.

A few years before Kiladjian graduated from high school, his father helped guide him toward the step that determined the rest of his life: coming to America.

"I liked the idea of studying in the U.S. My dad was seeing the political situation in Syria grow not as stable," he says. The late 1970s saw a Sunni challenge to the secular government and deepening Syrian military involvement in the Lebanese civil war. Since Kiladjian's father didn't have his own business to pass to his son, and Syria had a closed economy, his father knew it would be hard for him to find a job there.

"I think you should go," he told his son—the same advice he had given Kiladjian's older brother, who was studying dentistry in Indianapolis, where Kiladjian joined him in 1983. He arrived at Marion College without knowing English, but quickly learned enough to begin his studies.

"It was not a great experience in the Midwest. They didn't understand foreigners. There was a culture clash with us, coming with a different language, dark skin, and dark hair," he says. To make matters worse, the Beirut barracks bombing of October 1983 that killed 220 U.S. Marines was a fresh memory on campus. "If a group of us were talking in Arabic in the cafeteria, some students would say, 'You killed our Marines.' I just wanted to get out of Indiana," says Kiladjian, who left after one semester for Boston University's hotel management program.

"My mom always told me, 'You're good with people. You should go into hotel management,'" he says. The idea intrigued Kiladjian, who had enjoyed family stays in hotels. Boston "had a certain prestige" and a large Armenian population. His older brother joined him in his senior year, and they wound up living together until they both married.

In 1987 Kiladjian met his wife, Annie, an Armenian Canadian from Montreal whose family was from Egypt, and for the next four years they kept up a long-distance relationship while Kiladjian began his career. His first job, managing a new Boston-area restaurant for an Armenian restaurateur, taught him that he'd never have a life of his own if he continued in the restaurant side of the business. Burned out professionally, he nevertheless enjoyed his social life among his Armenian friends and dancing in a large Armenian folk-dance troupe called Sayat Nova that toured the U.S. and is still going strong.

Kiladjian landed his first hotel job, assistant housekeeping manager, at the luxury Boston Park Plaza Hotel, which led to higher-level jobs in several more hotels in the city. After visiting him and seeing how well he was doing, his father encouraged him to remain in the U.S. During his last year of college, Kiladjian had wanted to return home to Syria. "My dad really saw it clearly that I adapted well and spoke the language well. I just didn't see it," he says. In fact, a different choice soon presented itself: move to Montreal, where Annie lived. And in 1989, his own parents had retired there, uncertain about Syria's future.

"A lot of Middle Easterners think they need to plan ahead" in case of political trouble, says Kiladjian. Montreal made sense to his parents, since they were fluent in French and had two sons in Boston. But after just six months they returned to Damascus, where Kiladjian's sister lived, because they didn't like the hard-driving, car-dependent North American lifestyle, not to mention the climate. But two years later, Kiladjian himself moved to Montreal to marry Annie.

"It was a tough change, moving to Quebec, with a different language. I had to polish my French," he says. However, with all Annie's family in Montreal amid a large Armenian community, they enjoyed their life, and in 1993, their daughter was born. Kiladjian became a Canadian citizen and progressed along his career path at three different Montreal hotels.

"But I saw a better future for my career in the U.S.," he concluded after five years. With NAFTA coming into effect in 1994, he could get an annual work visa for the U.S., so he talked to his American contacts and landed a job within three weeks, at a Hilton in New Jersey with New Castle Hotels & Resorts, an upscale hotel-management company. The family moved there, and his son was born there in 1997. Next, Kiladjian began a professional odyssey that took him to a resort in northern Ontario, then to a hotel in Montreal, and finally, in 2000, to Portland, where he opened a new Hilton Garden Inn hotel at the Jetport.

"We moved here, we loved it, and I said, 'I'm not moving,'" he says. "We found this was the best place to stay for our kids to grow up," with laid-back people, a fine quality of life, good public schools in Portland, and proximity to Boston and Montreal. "The clincher was that it's on the ocean," says Kiladjian. Having settled in as a permanent resident with a green card, he is now on the path to U.S. citizenship.

With his appointment at the Portland Harbor Hotel, Kiladjian reached his professional goal. Under his management, the hotel has successfully weathered economic downturns, a noise issue with neighboring Old Port bars, and renovation. He recently oversaw the hotel's expansion into a new building next door. As chairman of the Convention and Visitors Bureau of Greater Portland, he exerts leadership in the wider business community.

And he has breathed new life into Maine's Armenian community. When Kiladjian founded the Armenian Cultural Association of Maine in 2002, he took over the organization of the state's estimated 2,000–3,000 second- and third-generation Armenians, of whom only a few Portland families still spoke Armenian.

"Armenians had a community here for many years, but their club members were getting older. So I decided to resurrect it after I moved here," he says. The association puts on several cultural events a year and has offered Armenian language classes for children. The group has also raised money for three orphanages and a hospital in Armenia. While Maine has no Armenian church, special holiday services are held at St. Paul's Anglican Church in Portland.

In Kiladjian's most concrete achievement on behalf of the community, he brought to completion in 2003 a project that had languished for years: a monument to Armenian genocide victims and Portland's Armenians at Cumberland Avenue and Franklin Arterial, once the center of the city's Armenian settlement. He has also helped organize annual multiethnic events at the University of Southern Maine to commemorate the genocides in Darfur, Cambodia, Rwanda, Armenia, and the Holocaust. He has met several times with Senators Susan Collins and Olympia Snowe as the state chair of the Armenian Assembly of America in its ongoing effort to persuade Congress to pass a resolution condemning the Armenian genocide. Each year, the Maine State Legislature recognizes the April 24 anniversary of the genocide, which Kiladjian's own parents never discussed. "They didn't want any attention. That community wanted to assimilate. They just wanted to live in peace," he says.

Kiladjian and his wife try to convey their Armenian heritage to their children by speaking the language and including them in cultural events. It helps that Annie's background closely matches his own; since her parents are Armenian from Egypt, she is familiar with Armenians' experience living among Arabs.

"I find it very important. Having the same background helps in many ways; a lot of the things we teach our kids, we're on the same page," he says. They have taken their children to the Middle East to expose them to ancient cultures there, to ride camels, and see Bedouins. "They're interested," he says, especially in the Armenian part of their heritage. The Kiladjian home is decorated with artwork celebrating their Armenian and Arab backgrounds, courtesy of Annie, who is an interior designer.

With several backgrounds to draw on, and after years of living in different countries, another person might have developed a confused identity by now. Not Kiladjian, who seems entirely at home with himself and his life, centered in family and community.

"My identity is Armenian—that's the language and culture," he says, adding that he was Syrian, too, when he was living there. "And now the U.S. is my home."

Grace Valenzuela

Grace Valenzuela, a small woman with an indefatigable spirit, carries some heavy burdens. As director of the Multilingual and Multicultural Center of Portland's public schools, she has to ensure that more than 1,500 students from fifty different countries learn academic English to succeed in school. As a community activist, she plays a key role in helping Maine meet the challenge of changing demographics. As the only person of color among school administrators wherever she goes in the overwhelmingly white state, she has to be a trailblazer.

"Whatever I do has to be more than just good, because whether I like it or not, most people see me as representing all professionals of color in my field. There's a huge burden of responsibility," she says.

Then why does she seem so lighthearted? Maybe it is because she loves her job. Maybe it is because she was born to responsibility and embraced it as a child in her native Philippines. Or maybe being named after Grace Kelly conferred a certain lightness of being.

It is not surprising that Valenzuela was named after a film star, since her family loved the movies. Lucky to have a relative who worked as projectionist in a movie theater, they never had to pay for a ticket to watch the Filipino or American movies. As a young girl, Valenzuela often volunteered to bring lunch to her cousin in the projection booth so that she could watch films from there, à la *Cinema Paradiso*.

Her American first name and Spanish last name actually represent the colonial history of the Philippines, she points out. Spain ruled the Southeast Asian archipelago of more than 7,000 islands from the sixteenth century to 1898, after which it was a U.S. territory until its independence in 1946. Her grandfather's sister, the family matriarch whom she called "Grandmother," chose the name Grace. "I was the first child in her household," where Valenzuela's parents were living, she explains.

Valenzuela was born in 1957 in Malabon, a coastal fishing town just northwest of Manila, the capital. Historically a trading center with a lot of Chinese influence, the town had an entrepreneurial, working-waterfront atmosphere in her childhood. She remembers gazing at fishponds as large as lakes as far as the eye could see, with their raised nets, walking paths, and fishing boats. Good smells emanated from a fish-sauce factory that produced the country's best *patis*, and the rich scent of ylang-ylang flowers, valued for making perfume, filled the air.

Everybody knew everybody's business in those days before the town became drawn into Manila's expanding metropolitan area, she says. In its population of various races, the main distinction that she felt between groups was class, partly because her own family was poor and did not own land. "The only soil we have is the soil in our shoes," her mother used to say.

Valenzuela's mother's parents died of starvation and TB during World War II, leaving her an orphan. Raised by older step-siblings, she could only attend school through the second grade because she had to take care of relatives' children. She learned how to read and write on her own.

Since Valenzuela's grandfather on her father's side had lost his share of the family's money, his nine children relied on relatives for help—especially Valenzuela's "grandmother," who had studied culinary arts in Europe and owned a large bakery. When Valenzuela's parents married, they moved into her big house, where her mother was treated like a daughter and sent to beauty school. Her father had to drop out of high school after two years to work at a canning factory, first as a line worker, and later as a mechanic. He worked such odd hours that Valenzuela rarely saw him.

When "Grandmother" died, the bakery became a hair salon, and Valenzuela's mother worked there as well in people's homes, often assisted by her daughter, from the age of seven.

"I hate having my hair done. I think it's because it reminds me of the chores I had to do at my mother's hair salon," says Valenzuela. As the oldest child, it also fell to her to take care of her five younger siblings, cook, and do the housework.

When she was eight years old, Valenzuela's family had to move to her mother's step-sister's house for a year—a sojourn she remembers vividly for the heady scent of gardenias and jasmine mixed with freshly brewed coffee wafting from the house as she sat on the front stoop staring at the nearby fishponds. In time, her parents got their own apartment, and although they were pinched economically, they sent her to a Roman Catholic private school until fifth grade, the year her buoyant self-confidence came up against a teacher who discriminated against her because she was poor.

"She would humiliate and embarrass me. That's when I first thought it was bad not to have money. I felt bad about myself," she says. Switching to a public school where an aunt of hers taught restored her spirits and exposed her to the role model in whose steps she would follow as a teacher. All in all, she feels she got an excellent education in both school systems, where English was the language of instruction.

At home, the family spoke Tagalog, the national language. Valenzuela taught herself to read it after she had learned to read English in school. Although there were newspapers at home, there was no money for books; for pleasure reading, she walked a mile to the public library every Saturday. A good language learner from a young age, she became an orator in sixth grade, relishing reciting poetry for an audience.

"When we had family gatherings, my mom would say, 'Grace, why don't you recite a poem for us?' It fell to me to carry the family torch. I wasn't shy," she says. The older relatives might not understand the English; they were more likely to know Spanish, a holdover from colonial days. Today, English and Filipino (a standardized version of Tagalog) are the official languages in the country of Malay–Polynesian-speaking peoples and a small minority of Chinese and other ethnic groups.

Never afraid to try something new, Valenzuela took off during the summertime to visit relatives, including the husband of her "grandmother," the man she credits with raising her while her parents worked. A former surgeon who had been traumatized by the Japanese during their World War II occupation, he suffered bouts of depression that kept him from practicing medicine, but he taught at a university.

"I didn't have educated parents, but he helped me with my homework. After I moved away, I would come back to his house, plan their menu for the week, and go to the market to do their shopping," says Valenzuela. She believes that carrying such responsibilities from the age of twelve helped prepare her for life.

"I'm an independent person. I have high confidence. I also was very expressive of my opinions. My mother was horrified sometimes," she says, adding that she never hesitated to fight for something she believed in. Her father worried, too. "You won't get a Filipino husband!" he warned.

But outspokenness was in the air in the 1960s, and political issues were discussed at school. "Teachers are political animals in the Philippines. They believe that teaching is a political act," she says. In high school, Valenzuela dreamed of becoming a journalist, but in 1972, when President Ferdinand Marcos declared martial law and clamped down on the press, she decided there was no future in journalism. Instead, she went to Philippine Normal College in Manila and became an English teacher. However, after teaching for three years in a girls' private school, she felt she wanted something more, and feared she would wind up like some of her colleagues who had been doing the same job for many, many years.

In 1980, Valenzuela's teacher aunt rescued her with news of a job teaching ESL in a United Nations refugee-processing center in Bataan, site of the infamous death march in World War II. Refugees streaming out of Southeast Asia received English and cultural training there before being sent to the U.S.

"I got the job, and a whole world opened to me," says Valenzuela, who took to the challenge of teaching adults learning English for survival and communicative competence and soon became a teacher supervisor. A diverse faculty lived in an international community of refugees, UN and U.S. State Department employees, and aid workers. She became a cultural broker, answering the Americans' questions in a setting where everyone seemed open-minded. "All of a sudden, there was a place for me. I didn't have to watch my words so carefully," she says.

Nor did her outspokenness get in the way of finding a husband. Three years later, at a conference in Toronto, she met a Connecticut Yankee, Val Hart, who was teaching ESL to adults in Portland and applying for a job in the Philippines. The two were married in 1984 in

Hong Kong, a place where neither of them had any connections.

"My condition for getting married was 'outside the country.' If I had married in the Philippines [a primarily Roman Catholic country], I couldn't get divorced if it didn't work out. Talk about long-term planning!" she laughs. Discovering they had to wait ten days in Hong Kong while the marriage notice was posted, they took off for a premarital honeymoon in China.

The couple lived for a time in Manila, he for work and she for graduate study. Although she was enjoying her life there, they decided to move to the U.S. for medical reasons when infertility issues got in the way of having a baby. In 1986, they arrived in Portland. Six years later, with Valenzuela's career well underway, their daughter was born.

Although Valenzuela had spent a year studying for her master's degree at the School for International Training in Brattleboro, Vermont, the first time she got to know "real" Americans outside an academic setting was in Maine. One of her first surprises was how little anyone knew about the Philippines, even the part U.S. soldiers had played there in World War II.

"They don't even know their own history," she thought. "If you're the dominant group, you don't have the need to know about other groups."

Another surprise was low voter turnout in elections. As soon as she arrived, she expedited her U.S. citizenship application, because she wanted to be part of the political process, including voting. In the Philippines, everyone talks politics, but she learned that is not always acceptable in the U.S., she says, recalling that her husband suggested she not bring up politics the first time she met his parents.

Valenzuela also found that American women were not treated as the strong women portrayed in the U.S. news media. Once, when she and her husband had a meeting with a bank manager in Maine, the manager directed all her attention to Valenzuela's husband—the opposite of what typically happened in the Philippines, where the women are in charge, she says.

"My stereotypes of Americans were debunked," she says, including the myth that there is no classism. "We don't talk about class. We want to think we're all equal." As for racism, she encountered it for the first time in her life in Maine, when she was followed in stores by security, and once when she was registering for a course for her teaching certification and was asked, "What kind of a name is Valenzuela? What kindergartener can pronounce that?" However, she felt luckier than many of the immigrants she helped settle into Maine's white culture.

"Unlike other people who come here by themselves, I had my husband, a white man, so in a tough situation, I could always use him," she says. Now she has several family members also living here. She had made an agreement with her parents that she wouldn't leave the Philippines if they didn't want to leave, too.

"I couldn't see myself having a child and not having my mother here," says Valenzuela, ever the long-term planner, aware that she would need childcare help. Her parents moved to Maine a few years after she did. Her father worked first in housekeeping at Portland's Holiday Inn, then as a custodian at Maine Medical Center. Two of her sisters live in Portland, one married to a Filipino and the other to a Vietnamese man she met here. Her brother is a medic in the U.S. Navy.

In 1987, Valenzuela started her first job in Maine at King Middle School in Portland, teaching ESL. Since then, she has trained teachers, designed and run programs, supervised an eighty-member multilingual staff, written curricula, created community networks—in short, everything it takes for English language learners to succeed in school.

Portland's schools still have only a handful of teachers of color. Low teacher pay and the area's small minority population create challenges in attracting them. Recently, the district, in partnership with USM, developed a teacher-training program for immigrants.

"This is the way to go," says Valenzuela. Already seeing rewards in hiring locally, she cites the example of a Somali who now teaches at Deering High School.

Despite the enormous challenge of teaching students who speak more than fifty languages, the Portland Public Schools' multilingual program ranks high nationally.

"We are a small state, but we can think out of the box, and because of our size, we can connect with each other much more easily than big states," says Valenzuela. She says funding agencies like Maine because start-up programs can be created quickly, without entrenched bureaucracies. For example, Valenzuela easily got a mental-health grant from the Robert Wood Johnson Foundation to provide access to mental-health services for immigrant children and their families, in partnership with community organizations, government agencies, and USM.

Valenzuela's impact on Maine's immigrants is incalculable, not only through her Portland schools work, but also as an advocate. She was a regular op-ed columnist for the *Portland Press Herald* in the late 1990s (an echo of her youthful dream of becoming a journalist). She is the co-founder and president of the Asian American Heritage Foundation and serves on the boards of LANA (Language Access for New Americans), the Immigrant Legal Advocacy Project, and in the Diversity Cabinet of United Way of Greater Portland. Over the years, she has worked with so many organizations devoted to civic leadership and social justice that the University of New England honored her in 2006 with a Deborah Morton Award for her distinguished career of public service.

A bicultural person, Valenzuela describes herself as "an Asian American from the Philippines." If, as she admits, "it's hard to be the only person of color all the time," she doesn't show it as she works to bring together immigrant and native-born Mainers to learn from each other.

"Every point of view that gets added to yours expands your worldview. Cross-cultural encounters are teaching and learning situations. I feel blessed by being in a role where I learn something every day from people whose cultural background is different from mine," she says.

Oscar Mokeme

It's hard to think of a better symbol of Maine's growing diversity than the Museum of African Culture in Portland. The only institution in northern New England focusing exclusively on sub-Saharan African arts and culture, it is also America's only African-owned museum, according to its Nigerian founder and director, Oscar Mokeme. At a time when large numbers of refugees and other immigrants from Africa have settled in the state, his once-struggling museum has come into its own.

Mokeme is a man of many parts, like some of the multifaceted tribal masks he brings to life in dance performances. Part collector, part educator, part healer, he transforms the artistry of West Africans and the wisdom of his ancestors into personal experiences American audiences can relate to. Whether explaining the artifacts in his museum or teaching about values to schoolchildren, Mokeme seeks to guide people to self-knowledge and a better life.

When the decade-old museum moved in 2008 from Spring Street into new, expanded quarters on Brown Street, near the Portland Museum of Art and Maine College of Art, it took its place in the arts district as a respected contributor to the state's cultural life. In the wider community, Mokeme forms artistic collaborations with local museums, the Museum of Fine Arts in Boston, and others; conducts hundreds of educational programs; and leads colorful public celebrations such as Portland's springtime Ram Parade. He also provides a nexus for traditional African and contemporary African and African American artists through his Black Artists Forum gallery at the museum.

To walk into the small museum, redolent of exotic woods anointed with herbal waters, is to enter a kind of spirit world where costumed, life-sized figures and elaborately carved wooden masks welcome you, wearing such intense facial expressions that you feel as if they are speaking to you. And that, of course, is the intent. In Mokeme's culture of the Igbo people of southeastern Nigeria, they speak truths to those who listen.

"In Christianity, these were once considered idols," says Mokeme, whose ability to interpret them to help others was honed during the apprenticeship he served as a descendant of a long line of priests, as well as in years of formal university study. "The psychology and motivation behind the art interests me. They are not just art; they are documents where ancient wisdom was recorded."

About 150 of the 1,500-plus artifacts in the collection remain on permanent display in the museum's three small rooms painted in welcoming earth tones. They include ivory, jewelry, musical instruments, wooden stools, textiles, pottery, and bronzes—some dating back 3,000 years. Many of the museum's holdings are Igbo. Others are from Nigeria's Yoruba ethnic group, or other African countries. These ceremonial, decorative, and archeological artifacts are only a fraction of the thousands Mokeme owns; the rest are stored in his parents' home in Nigeria.

The startling masks take center stage. One, a spirit mask made for Mokeme's initiation ceremony when he was twelve years old, features a star on its forehead (signifying that he would travel far, but return home) and a heart on its chin (indicating love, gentleness, and humanitarianism). Its two upright horns foretold the self-motivation and gift of motivating others that can be seen in Mokeme's work. Horns figure prominently in the masks. Some symbolize strength and determination. Other, curved-in horns warn that one's misbehavior will bounce back on him. The oldest mask dates to 1600 A.D.

Through the centuries, the masks, which are primarily made and worn by men, have been used for rites of passage, marriages, funerals, and ceremonies involving agriculture or honoring ancestors. The carved wooden faces are adorned with cowrie shells, fibers, and/or fabric. Worn in masquerades along with elaborate costumes, they convey moral lessons. In a discussion with teens, Mokeme might use the masks to teach about anger, peer pressure, and family dynamics. In a nursing home, he might explore end-of-life issues. He may point to curved-in horns to show that people do not have to fight if they are provoked to anger, but can return harmful energy to the sender.

Much of Mokeme's work also involves healing, whether he is talking to groups about community values, or giving a private blessing at the museum's shrine. In the Igbo culture, it is a priest's job to divine messages from the spirits about how to live a worthy life. He takes his role as healer seriously, having been tapped for it at an early age. Born in 1960 to Igbo parents, he learned healing arts in the village of Aborji, in southeastern Nigeria, where his ancestors had practiced them for thousands of years, he says.

"My father was a civil engineer by training, but by gift he was a medicine man/healer. We have a very ancient shrine, and people come to get treatment," he says. Mokeme apprenticed with his grandfather, who lived in the family compound. The compound had a meeting hall where people sought comfort for the pain of various problems and were guided to heal through application of herbs, medicine, and water. Mokeme, who was the eighth of nine children, was taught at the age of three to carry water from a nearby river to the shrine, a role reserved for a young boy destined to become a dibia, or healer. His siblings had other functions at the shrine, for example, mixing herbs; all were healers, and in fact two have become medical doctors.

"Every child has a particular gift," says Mokeme, whose own gift was identified as "understanding the spirits." Once an ability is recognized by the elders, the child moves through proscribed steps in training so that he always knows his function, he says, contrasting his upbringing with that of American children, who at twenty-one may still not know who they are or what their role is. This home of powerful traditional culture was also a Christian household wherein the family's spirituality embraced both worlds, as is common among Igbos. Mokeme's mother, who worked as a nurse and later as a subcontractor with her husband, came from a missionary family whose ancestors had built the first Anglican church in the region.

Although born and raised in the large city of Aba, Mokeme spent a lot of time in his hometown, Aborji Oba, apprenticing with elders who trained him to interpret dreams, communicate with nature, and perform traditional rituals. By the time he was a teenager, he was practicing healing rituals. Mokeme's parents sent him to Christian boarding schools, after which he was expected to work for a year "to get a taste of life and hardship," then travel for a year. His travels began at sixteen, when he won a World Health Organization essay contest that funded a trip to England, which led to discovery of his mission in life. In a London museum, he saw African art on display for the first time and realized its worth in a different context, esteemed by Europeans. Someday, he thought, he would open his own museum, and on his return to Nigeria, he began collecting.

"When a medicine man died, I'd go to buy shrine objects and carry them back to my family-owned shrine," he says. "I got fired up about protecting and preserving art." Meanwhile, he worked at various jobs—a year in a post office, followed by three years in a bank—and returned to England to study business. In travels around Europe, he began trading, sometimes selling an Italian shoe manufacturers' shoes for him on London streets. The manufacturer even named a shoe after him, "the Oscar," which sold well in Nigeria.

"I paid my dues," says Mokeme, whose travel experiences inspired him to go to college in the U.S. After considerable research, he chose Massachusetts because he liked the sound of its name and because "I thought the Kennedys were there, and if something happened to me, they would save me," he laughs. He was anything but naïOve, however; in fact, he felt that his worldview was advanced compared to his fellow students at Mt. Ida College in Newton, and later at the University of Massachusetts/Boston, where he studied business administration. From the time he arrived in the U.S. at nineteen, he felt comfortable, having come with the maturity of one who had paid his own way and knew who he was. So it came as a shock to hear the term "colored people" for the first time.

"I began to see the degradation of human dignity," says Mokeme, who felt somewhat insulated from racial discrimination by the ancestral pride he brought with him, summed up in the way he identifies himself: "I'm an Igbo man." He felt he came to the U.S. as someone with substance to offer the community, and that was literally true. "I carried my masks in my bag when I first came to the U.S. My professors would ask about them and I'd talk about my art and my life." Soon he was earning pocket money for his speeches. Later, he examined African art through different, academic lenses, earning a B.A. in humanities from Southern New Hampshire University and an M.A. in psychology from Union Institute. Putting together his traditional training and university studies eventually brought him full circle.

"I realized my calling was back to my roots," he says. "My role became to use the art to understand 'Who are you?'" His knowledge of psychology helped him use his healing abilities—for instance, to combat what he saw as a "spiritual bankruptcy" in American society, especially among young people. As a young apprentice to his grandfather, watching him bless masks brought to the family shrine, he had gained an awareness of the power of the ritual objects within his culture. Now that he held a deeper understanding of them, he could see their benefits for any culture, and his role as a moral educator and healer took shape.

Serendipity brought him to the unlikely place where Mokeme would realize both his potential as a teacher/healer and his youthful dream of opening a museum: the state of Maine. One day, having misplaced his train ticket for a ride from New York to Boston, Mokeme found a stranger paying the fare for him and introducing himself as Peter Erskine, owner of Mexicali Blues, a Portland import shop. With a shared interest in collecting art, the two formed a friendship that brought Mokeme to Portland in 1989. Struck by the city's wealth of art, he visited galleries and the Portland School of Art (now Maine College of Art) and started thinking about what he might be able to contribute.

"What if you combined contemporary and traditional art?" he wondered.

Soon after, he moved to Portland with $436 in his pocket and went directly to the Chamber of Commerce to ask for help starting a janitorial service—a line of work he had to be taught, since it was considered beneath a highborn Igbo man like himself when he was growing up. The business, along with a break on rental space from a local realtor, eventually funded the first stage of his museum dream—a gallery and import shop, where he worked by day after cleaning at night. It wasn't easy to build a following; he found that a lot of Mainers in the 1980s had never been exposed to international culture. "People would look in and see a black man and not come in," he says.

Mokeme got help with the second stage of his dream when Art Aleshire, a Hannaford executive with a love of African art, stopped by his gallery and struck up a friendship. Aleshire wound up offering financial support, and together they co-founded the Museum of African Culture in 1998. Besides art, Mokeme and Aleshire had another shared passion. On visits to Africa, Aleshire had become interested in medicine. On Mokeme's frequent visits to Nigeria, he had often brought donations of medical supplies to doctors. Their twin interests meshed, and Mokeme has been working at the nonprofit museum every day since then, without pay.

He travels widely to conduct educational programs both here and abroad, working with hundreds of teachers, childcare professionals, college art departments, corporations, and even jail staffs. He leads workshops on healing for doctors and psychiatrists interested in alternative approaches to medicine. For the general public, he uses music, dance, storytelling, and traditional Igbo masquerades to challenge viewers to consider who they are as individuals and as members of society. The museum also shows weekly films and operates an educational resource center that includes a lending library of books, videos, and touch kits.

On occasion, Mokeme takes his cultural messages to the street in joyous rituals like the annual Ram Parade celebrating the arrival of spring. On Palm Sunday, he dresses in an enormous ram mask and costume and leads people beating drums and carrying giant hand-made puppets through Portland neighborhoods. At another ritual, the New Moon Festival, participants pledge to reach a certain personal goal by the next new moon.

One theme in Mokeme's programs is the importance of culture in helping people understand diversity—a theme that resonates with white Mainers adjusting to the state's recent wave of newcomers from ethnicities and societies very different from their own. And to recent immigrants finding their way in a new culture, Mokeme offers an example of an immigrant who has thrived in Maine while retaining his African identity. Wearing his distinctive red cap, signifying that he is a tribal chief of distinction, he moves easily within and beyond ethnic borders, spreading his spiritual message with the authority of one who holds the priesthood title of *The Ugo-Orji the first, the Ozo-Dimani of Aborji Oba.*

"I feel there's an energy here. That's the reason I'm here, to serve the community and glorify God's name," says Mokeme, who acknowledges how much his new home has given him by believing in his dream of bringing an African culture museum to Maine.

"This is the work of friends, the community, a lot of black artists, who have all gone out of their way to sustain us," says Mokeme. To ensure the museum's future, he has established an endowment fund through the Maine Community Foundation. More and more people find in Mokeme's art collection and teachings an exciting and deeply affecting cultural experience. For his part, Mokeme says he feels blessed. "What I have found in Maine is friendship and a community of love."

VAN AND KIM LUU

With every gleaming hardwood floor Van Luu lays, he puts a little more distance between himself and his tough childhood in Vietnam at the close of the war. He takes pride in the high quality of his craftsmanship, mastered in a society where most educational and work opportunities were closed to him as the Amerasian son of a Vietnamese mother and an American G.I. father.

Van and his wife Kim have built a successful business, A-Z Floor Sanding, in southern Maine. At job sites, they put in long hours together, installing, stripping, sanding and repairing floors. At home, in their spacious South Portland house with ballroom-quality floors, they are raising their four children to value the good fortune their industriousness has brought the family. "Mom and Dad came here with an empty hand. Can you imagine how we got like this? You have to appreciate what you have," they like to tell them.

The story of how they got to be where they are begins with war, love, and U.S. immigration policy. Van was born in 1970, five years before the war ended, and grew up in Da Nang, in the middle of the country. He was the third of four children, the only one whose father was an American soldier; his mother was married to a Vietnamese. She was a homemaker who supplemented the family's income during the war by cooking at a servicemen's club on the city's large American air base. Van never met his father, but was told his name and saw a picture of him.

Certain memories of Van's early life are hard for him to erase. "We saw airplanes flying, people running, Viet Cong coming, rocket fire," he recalls. Two of his uncles died in the fighting. After the war ended, a more personal threat emerged, as he grew old enough to become aware that he was different from other children.

"When I look at you, you are half and half, and you don't look like me," he would hear. Amerasian children were often taunted with crude racist names and attacked with sticks and stones, so that they themselves felt ashamed. "Society abandoned families involved with Americans," because the Vietnamese associated them with the defeated U.S. soldiers and were angry at women who had had relationships with them, Van explains.

Most mothers of Amerasians, like Van's, worked on or near U.S. bases and met lonely American men who could help support them for a time. Few of the liaisons resulted in marriage, and the women's relatives and neighbors ostracized them. When Saigon fell to the Viet Cong and the North Vietnamese army in 1975, the situation of Amerasians and their mothers deteriorated, because the new Communist government regarded such women as collaborators and denied their offspring educational and vocational opportunities.

Van's family lived essentially as outcasts, with no man of the house; his stepfather died of sickness when Van was eight. Barred from access to public schools, he and his siblings were lucky to be taken in by nuns at a Roman Catholic school, where he studied up to the seventh grade. Even attending the church school was fraught with risk.

"You cannot go outside—somebody hit you. You stay home. Church help me, taught me carpentry. Wait for sundown, go home when not many people around," says Van (whose work schedule has never allowed him time to perfect his English; Kim helps by translating). At church, starting at the age of seven, Van learned the trade that would propel him forward in life. Along with another Amerasian boy, he chopped down trees, milled them into lumber, and became highly skilled at making cabinets and furniture.

Meanwhile, to the south in the Mekong Delta, Kim Nguyen was growing up under a similar fate. She was born in 1974, the year before the war ended, in An Giang Province, a flat, rice-growing region of canals and small rivers. Like Van's family, hers was shunned because an American G.I. had fathered her older brother. Her mother knew English, having gone to an American school. The only girl in her wealthy family, she was spoiled, preferring hanging out and having fun to thinking about her future, says Kim. The first man in her life was an American, and when the war ended, so did her relationship with him. Kim heard from relatives that he had asked her mother to come with him, but the family had refused.

"After the American father, we had two different fathers, bad guys, but no fathers in the house, ever. My mom so suffered," Kim says. Isolated socially, her mother had to do what many others in her position did—hire out as an agricultural laborer.

"People treated my mom and older brother bad. My mom was always working for other people in the rice fields. My family was very poor, and the area was very poor," says Kim. They lived in the fields, but didn't own any land. If they ever could have had access to the family wealth, that chance disappeared when Kim's grandfather died and his family lost everything in the war.

As the third of ten children, Kim took care of her younger siblings, along with other duties. By the time she was five years old, she was harvesting rice and bringing home fish from the river. Since they didn't have enough to eat, let alone to pay school fees, she had to drop out of school after the third grade. She watched as other children passed by, wearing nice clothes on their way to school, while she headed off to work in the fields.

"It's sad, but we were used to it. So we don't feel any emotion. We have to live with it. I look at my mom—don't cry and suffer; accept. If we don't accept it, what we do? Wait for a miracle?" Still, sometimes she would sit in the bushes, looking at the sky, wondering what was up there—always dreaming, she remembers.

Then, one day, a kind of miracle did occur. The U.S. government, long gone from the country it had sent so many servicemen and women to, and lost, woke up to the plight of the Amerasian children left in the war's wake. In 1988, Congress passed the Amerasian Homecoming Act, giving special priority status to Vietnamese Amerasians and their close relatives to immigrate to the U.S. With the "golden passport," families got their transportation expenses paid and were awarded refugee entitlement benefits on arrival.

The law came after years of postwar refusals by U.S. governments to accept responsibility for Amerasians, and an official policy of discouraging U.S. servicemen from marrying Vietnamese nationals. It wasn't until the 1980s, when journalists visiting Ho Chi Minh City (the former Saigon) reported on Amerasian children begging in the streets, that support for their immigration built across the U.S. and reached Congress. Looking back today on that policy reversal, Kim believes it came about because good-hearted American servicemen's consciences began to bother them. She pictures them thinking, "I have children there. I have to do something to help."

Kim's mother heard about the new program, but couldn't afford to travel to a big city to apply, so she filled out papers locally and then waited. In 1991, their chance finally came. The family traveled to Ho Chi Minh City and settled into the Amerasian Transit Center, a short-term residential facility constructed near the airport. There, U.S. consular officials interviewed applicants to determine if the children really had American fathers, reviewing proof such as the child's birth date and the name of the father. "During the interview, Americans can see the children are half and half," says Kim.

Kim was seventeen. At the center, she met a young man from Da Nang, Van Luu, in the crowd of applicants, and they hit it off. After just a few hours together, Van and Kim had to say good-bye, but they exchanged information about where their families were being sent and agreed to write each other. Since both their families were Catholic, they were on their way to places where Catholic agencies had sponsored them and would oversee their resettlement—Des Moines, where her family had relatives, in Kim's case, and Philadelphia in Van's. First, though, they were sent to a refugee-processing center in the Philippines for six months of language and cultural-orientation classes.

Once in Iowa, rather than go to high school, Kim did what she had done throughout her childhood—work. She joined an assembly line of older Vietnamese women working in a cold meatpacking plant.

"I just think about work, not about education," she says.

Van, too, could not afford to go to school once he arrived in Philadelphia, so after just two weeks of English classes, he got a job assembling aluminum patio furniture. "The work was good," he says. At twenty-one, he knew he would have to make his own way, using the one skill he knew. He didn't try to find his American father; like the overwhelming majority of Amerasians, he was never to be reunited with him. A friend of his father's later told Van that he had died.

In their separate new lives, Van and Kim each had the same initial reaction to America:

"Compared with my country, I like," says Van.

"We have freedom. No one control us. Nice people here," Kim sums up.

Six months into his life in Philadelphia, Van heard from an Amerasian friend with whom he had worked in Vietnam doing carpentry and cabinetmaking. The friend, who had come to Maine a few months earlier, recommended Portland and invited Van to come. Leaving his family behind, Van moved to Portland and made Barber Foods his first stop, like so many other refugees before him. He worked at the chicken-processing plant only six weeks, however, before saying to himself, "I have a skill I can use." Through a friend in Chelsea, Massachusetts, he got into the flooring business, working there and in Maine.

By then, Kim had joined him. They had continued to write to each other during their first year in America, and when Van wrote, "Portland is good, come here," she came. Like him, she went straight to Barber Foods and got another cold, assembly-line job like the one she left in Des Moines, but one with good pay and benefits and a welcoming atmosphere. She took English classes at Portland Adult Education, progressing well, and the young couple began to find their footing, working hard and meeting new challenges together.

"At that time in Maine, nobody had a good flooring company," says Van. Eventually, when a Vietnamese entrepreneur started one, Van's expert craftsmanship was what he needed. After several years of working for him, Van decided to strike out on his own. He and Kim started their flooring business in 1999, the second such Vietnamese-owned company; since then, at least six more have opened in the greater Portland area. Kim works alongside Van at job sites and handles administration, using English and business skills learned at Portland Adult Education.

At home, their older children, thirteen and twelve, take care of the younger ones, three and one and a half, doing their part for the family. If Kim has a criticism of American society, it is that some children become spoiled in the child-centered culture. To make sure her children value what they have, she reminds them of how hard it was for Van and her growing up in Vietnam. "I have to explain, 'You have a good life. You can't have it all,'" she says.

If Kim and Van seem relieved to have put their life in Vietnam behind them and focus strictly on the good things America has to offer, it is little wonder. Unlike many other refugees who led contented lives amid supportive extended families until calamity struck their homelands, Amerasians' rejection by their own cultures added an additional layer of suffering to the one all Vietnamese experienced during and immediately following the long war.

"We still miss and remember Vietnam, but also it's painful for us," says Kim. "We're really happy over here."

ZEYNEP TURK

Let's say your small medical supplies business is doing well nationally, and you want to expand into overseas markets, but don't know where to begin. One day, you happen to walk by the Maine International Trade Center's glass-walled office in downtown Portland and decide to stop in. Chances are, senior trade specialist Zeynep Turk will help you get started. As her name suggests, she is from Turkey. Growing up in Istanbul, the historic trading crossroads of East and West, would seem to make her a natural for this profession. With her M.B.A. and strong banking background, she could practice it in her booming native city or many other cities in the world.

So you may wonder: Why Maine?

Turk's choice of Portland was more an evolution than a conscious decision to immigrate. From her student days on the small campus of the University of Maine at Machias to her present job, one step just led to another on a successful career path, to the point where today she is in a key position to help move the state forward economically. Along the way, she realized she had adapted happily to Maine, even though it couldn't be more different from her faraway homeland.

The great metropolis of Istanbul straddles two continents, Europe and Asia. It was spreading so fast during Turk's youth that by now it is Europe's largest city. She was born in 1969 in the Gayreteppe neighborhood, on the European side of the city. Not as densely populated then as it is now, fields appeared here and there amid the cramped streets carrying exotic smells and the sounds of many languages. From one of the city's restaurant rooftop terraces, Turk could gaze at the minarets of the fabled Aya Sofya, the Blue Mosque, and the mosque of Suleyman the Magnificent, or look out over Topkapi Palace to the sparkling waters of the Bosphorus Strait, with its ships arriving from all over the world. She could explore one of the vast bazaars for clothing or Turkish delicacies, or stop in a carpet shop for a leisurely chat over a glass of tea.

An only child, Turk lived in an apartment house with her parents, who were middle- to upper-middle class. Her father was a banker who had grown up in Isparta, in the Mediterranean region. His own father had been an elementary-school teacher, and his three siblings had also become professionals. Turk's mother came from an Ankara family; her father was a military judge. Although both her grandmothers were housewives, and her own mother was a housewife who did volunteer work, Turk was destined for a professional career because of her parents' strong emphasis on her education and their modern attitude about daughters.

"My parents wanted me to stand on my own feet. They wanted me to have a career," she says. Furthermore, they encouraged her to enter any field she wanted to, even if it was male-dominated, like her father's banking profession. "Their attitude was, 'You can do it.'" Girls in Istanbul's secular Muslim society were not held back by religious strictures, either, and Turk's parents were less observant Muslims than her devout grandparents.

"I always felt comfortable being secular," says Turk, who drinks alcohol and eats pork. "I still pray, in my own way." When Turk was born, the modern democratic state founded by Mustafa Kemal, known as Ataturk ("father of the Turks"), was only forty years old, but his secular reforms were entrenched. Today that tradition is under challenge from Islamic influences.

"Being a secular Turk, you're torn. It makes you cautious about being judged by the more religious crowd," she says. "Turkey can be ultramodern and ultraconservative. It can be a clash sometimes." To Americans grown accustomed to news coverage of fundamentalist Muslim sects, Turkey's religious freedom and secular public life offer a unique view of Islam—one Turk wishes more people could see: "There's such a harsh perception of Muslims with radical Islam that I want to make the point that not all Muslims are radical."

As a child, Turk spent most of her time playing in the small yard of her apartment house, enjoying school, and exploring the city. Her life was tranquil, despite periods of government instability in the country (she has memories of running to the store to buy bread before curfew during a military coup in 1980). It was an unhurried childhood that she looks back on as unlike that of American children, or at least those in outdoorsy Maine.

"I don't know how to ride a bicycle. The kids here all ski and bike, and the parents do, too," says Turk, to whom it sometimes seems that American kids aren't allowed to relax enough. Even today, her idea of a fun weekend is not the L.L. Bean image of donning a heavy backpack and going climbing. In her upbringing, socializing trumped outdoor recreation. "We would visit friends and family to eat, drink, and be merry." She thrived on the love and support of her two parents until she was thirteen years old and her father died, leaving her mother and her to support each other emotionally.

"It made me grow up faster," says Turk. She and her mother dealt with their sadness silently, and as they got on with life, her mother continued to encourage Turk to do well at school so she could get a career. "Stand on your own feet. Don't rely on marriage" was her message. Turk studied hard, winning admittance to the same prestigious Arnavutkoy high school where Nobel laureate Orhan Pamuk had studied. But there was fun, too—hanging out with friends, dating, a trip to New York City with her mother. Then, in her junior year, she spent a summer in Japan on an exchange program where she got to know teens from different countries, and her horizons widened even more.

"After being an only child, that changed me. I was on cloud nine," says Turk, who gives her mother a lot of credit for letting her go, especially since the trip stimulated a desire to go to the U.S. for college, leaving her mother alone once again.

"I thought it would be good for me to be on my own. I never thought I'd stay," she says. Turk chose the University of Maine at Machias because it was reasonably priced, showed happy faces in the catalog, and was located at what looked to her on the map as "right over Boston." The small down-east campus turned out to be an excellent choice for Turk because she didn't get lost in the crowd and wound up making a solid contribution, working in the campus pluralism office and founding the International Student Club. Rather than return home after college, Turk followed an Australian friend to the University of Maine at Orono for graduate school, made affordable by her job as a resident director.

"Orono was the logical next step. I thought, 'Two more years, then I'll go back to Turkey,'" she says. Instead, Key Bank recruited her for a management trainee program when she graduated with her M.B.A., and she signed on for a one-year extension of her student visa. Starting in Augusta, Turk rotated to various banks in Maine and New Hampshire. "It was just enough to give you a taste. It was sort of like being a tourist," she says. She discovered that she liked private banking, where she could use her people skills. After exploring other banking jobs and interviewing with a bank in Istanbul on a trip home, Turk decided to get a green card and work longer in the U.S., with the thought that she would return to Turkey if things didn't work out.

"The longer you stay away, the harder it is to go back," says Turk, who by then had many close friends in Maine. Since Key Bank wasn't sponsoring green cards, she took an underwriting job with TD Banknorth, which did sponsor her. "Number crunching" not being her favorite type of work, she was delighted when the bank loaned her to United Way of Greater Portland, where she worked for two years as a fundraiser. "It was good experience, but hard work," a high-pressure sales job with nonprofit wages, says Turk. So, when she heard of an opening at Maine International Trade Center in 2005, she jumped at it. The center, a public–private partnership, is the state's only trade assistance organization, with a mission to help businesses expand overseas. For someone with her background and love of working with people, the job as senior trade specialist was perfect for Turk.

"If you travel to Turkey and you want to sell carpets here, you come to us and say, 'Where do I begin?' We give you information and contact names. We do market research and trade shows. We help with imports and exports. Our goal is economic development for Maine," she says. With a staff of just eight people, the center offers free technical assistance, international credit reports, and import-export counseling to any business on its first stop at MITC, and advises businesses paying a membership fee for longer periods of time.

With hot markets such as China and Vietnam opening up, and the value of the dollar falling, Maine exports rose in 2008, and more Maine businesses were taking advantage of the center's services, which include sponsoring conferences on topics like Women in Global Leadership and Vietnam's Roaring Economy. Traditional Maine products like seafood, wood products, pulp paper, and semiconductors do well overseas, and the biotech industry is increasing its exports—for example, of medical diagnostic test-kit components.

"I like the whole international dimension. We get to look for new markets and travel. If you do take a company overseas to a trade show and they make a connection, you feel great," says Turk, who also appreciates working in Portland, a livelier place than her previous work sites. She likes it that for her job, she always has to be aware of what's going on in the world, and she is surrounded by people who share her global curiosity. Asked if she finds Maine people internationally minded, she says she doesn't believe that comes naturally, unless they need to be, say for business, or because they have a child going abroad. And how curious are Mainers about her own country?

"Not everyone asks," although her friends are interested in Turkey, she says. With more news reports about Turkey's tourism boom and economic resurgence, Americans' views of her country are changing for the better, she believes, judging from reactions when people learn she is Turkish.

"My experience used to be, 'Oh, I've seen *Midnight Express,*'" she says, referring to the 1978 film whose unflattering and distorted picture of Turkey offered one of the few representations of her country in popular culture at the time. She used to meet Mainers who were surprised to learn that Turkey was not a land of deserts and camels. Today, however, Americans have access to a range of internationally respected Turkish writers, artists, and musicians (although Turkey's best athletic achievements, in wrestling and weight lifting, find little interest abroad). One writer in particular, Orhan Pamuk, is widely read in the U.S., but remains controversial in Turkey for calling the 1915 massacre of Armenians "genocide," a term unrecognized by the Republic of Turkey. While Turk enjoys reading Pamuk's many-layered novels and believes it is good that he explores harsh realities, she hopes readers will be open to other points of view on the Armenian question.

"Growing up, you heard different things. Atrocities happened, but they happened on both ends [by Armenians and by Turks]. I'm one of those Turks who wouldn't accept the term 'genocide'. I've been in situations where I've felt attacked" on the issue, she says, adding that she has had positive experiences with the Armenians she knows in this country.

Turk finds commonalities with other immigrants in Maine and tries to help those learning English by serving on an ESL scholarship committee offering financial assistance for higher education. One of the things she likes about the U.S. is its liberal educational system, where students have more flexible study paths than in Turkey. Looking around her at Portland's growing population of refugees, she feels lucky to have come to Maine the way she did—by choice.

Turk is proud of her home country, and has even become more "nationalistic" about it as a result of being an immigrant, she thinks. She misses her family, the comfort of speaking her native language, the food, the climate, and the wonderful memories of her youth.

"Missing Turkey is like missing my childhood," she says, wondering if nostalgia has begun to color her impressions. "I also miss certain kinds of energy in Istanbul, but if I lived there, it would probably wear me out," she laughs. Yet in choosing to remain in the U.S., she has given up a lot: more time with her mother and extended family, a more settled life, and an easier emotional road. "You give up that wholeness," is how she describes it.

Even so, Turk thinks she will stay in Maine, where she recently bought a home. "On the other hand, I'm aware of realities like my mom getting older. We'll have to see how things work out," she says. Turk plans to become a U.S. citizen, in which case she will hold dual citizenship here and in Turkey. With only about fifteen other Turks in southern Maine, she will continue to be in a small minority, but the many American and international friends she has made over the years sustain her, reinforcing the cosmopolitan person she has become.

"I'm definitely a Turk. I don't want to lose that identity. But I see America as a second home," she says. As westernized as she is, certain Turkish habits persist, and are likely to comfort her for years to come. One is exchanging her shoes for slippers at the door of her home. Another is hanging amulets against the evil eye in her house. "I believe in that," says Turk. So far, they seem to have worked.

Emrush Zeqiri

The first thing you see when you enter the Zeqiri family's Portland living room are two huge flags hanging on the wall side by side: the familiar Stars and Stripes and a less familiar one with a black, double-headed eagle on a blood-red field—the historic banner of the ethnic Albanians of Kosovo. Every November 28th, Emrush Zeqiri gathers together his family and other members of Maine's tiny community of Albanian Kosovars on Albanian Flag Day to celebrate the flag for which he was once arrested in his homeland.

During Zeqiri's youth in what was then a Serb-dominated autonomous province of Yugoslavia, Zeqiri held to such symbols with a passion rooted in a proud identity as one of Kosovo's more than 90 percent ethnic Albanians, who speak their own language and feel a close kinship with other Albanians scattered in enclaves throughout Serbia, Macedonia, and Montenegro. While most are nominally Muslim, some are Christians; however, Zeqiri adheres to neither religion.

"I am Albanian!" he says, and it soon becomes clear what defending that identity has cost him.

Born in 1964 in Kokaj, a village on the Kosovo–South Serbian border, Zeqiri was one of seven children. His father, like many others in the impoverished region, had to leave home to support his family, laboring in an Austrian metalworking factory for twenty-six years and coming home only twice a year.

"He sacrificed his life for us," says Zeqiri. "I feel sad whenever I think about him." From his father, mother, and two uncles who lived with the family and kept a close watch on the children, Zeqiri acquired his strong work ethic and sense of male responsibility.

"I was the first boy born in my family. I had some privilege," says Zeqiri, who absorbed the cultural message that a son should go to school, get a good job, and later take care of his parents. His mother spent a lot of time teaching her children, and Zeqiri loved learning. Although the family was not as badly off economically as some, life wasn't easy for him as a child. In the one pair of shoes he got each year, he walked four miles along muddy roads to the bus stop for elementary school. To get to high school, he awoke at 3:00 a.m. and walked thirteen miles to the nearby Serbian town of Presheva, another Albanian enclave.

After Zeqiri graduated in 1983, he fulfilled his compulsory military obligation for the next year. Since Albanians had begun protesting Serbian control of the province, relations between Serbs and Albanians were tense. As one of only two Albanians in his army battalion, he was told to stay away from his compatriot and not speak Albanian. In fact, Zeqiri knew little Serbo-Croatian at the time; his Albanian teachers had taught the Cyrillic alphabet and some poems, but not much else about the language.

"The Serbs called us irredentists," he says, referring to a notion that Kosovo's Albanians longed to reclaim the wider ancestral territory they inhabited before World War I, including Albania itself. In fact, Zeqiri had never been to neighboring Albania and even today expresses little interest in it. After his army years, he discovered how wide the ethnic gulf had become when he went to Pristina, the capital, to attend university, with its majority Albanian student body.

"It was two worlds, Serbs and Albanians," says Zeqiri, who studied philosophy and sociology. He struggled to learn amid poor conditions, waiting hours in line to get into the library and studying in a basement with no heat. Following student protests in May 1988, Serb police began cracking down, according to Zeqiri. "I saw police killing students" for shouting slogans such as "Democracy!" "Freedom!" and "Kosovo—Republic!" he says.

In 1989, Serbian President Slobodan Milosevic revoked Kosovo's autonomy, banned news reports in the Albanian language, placed Serbs in Albanians' jobs, and purged high schools and universities of Albanians, who set up an underground educational system in families' homes. Kosovo, already the poorest part of Yugoslavia, slid further into poverty, and unemployment skyrocketed. Although Zeqiri had completed his course work, he could not sit for exams, so he returned to his village and continued to study for them.

"I had hope. We all thought, 'It's not going to be like this forever,'" he says. He and other Albanians began quietly organizing in the eastern Kosovo town of Gjilan, where his family built a house in 1990 near his mother's relatives. Guarding his banned Albanian language books and flag, Zeqiri took part in political discussions and protests against growing persecution of ethnic Albanians. For the next five years, he moved back and forth between Gjilan and his home in Kokaj, finding occasional work as a car mechanic. He married in 1991, and two daughters were born in the next few years. Meanwhile, he continued his political activism, until one day in May of 1995.

"I had just come back from Gjilan. About 4:00 a.m., my house was circled by fifteen special Serbian police and an Albanian inspector. A police put a handgun to my forehead, and another put one in my back. They asked me about weapons and beat me in front of my family. I didn't have weapons. They took me to a police station in Presheva. I had two ribs broken, my left eye swollen, and trouble breathing. I stayed there ten hours; then they said, 'Sorry, we were looking for another person.' It wasn't true; they just wanted to hurt me." When he tried to get X-rays of his ribs at a hospital, a doctor refused, fearing to supply documentation of police abuse.

Charged with illegally celebrating Albanian Flag Day and owning Albanian books, Zeqiri was sentenced to three years in prison, reduced to one year after he signed a confession.

He was imprisoned in the south Serbian city of Leskovac for most of the next year, missing the birth of his first son. The only Albanian among a population of Serb criminals, he was once accused of stealing from another prisoner. However, a sympathetic Serb prisoner vouched for his innocence and told Zeqiri, "Trust me, one day Kosovo will be a republic." Once out of prison, Zeqiri returned to his village, where his family, labeled as "nationalists," remained under police watch.

In early 1998, Zeqiri was able to return to Pristina and finish his university exams, as mounting frustration among Kosovo's Albanians led to fighting between the Kosovo Liberation Army (KLA) and Serb authorities. Sporadic attacks turned into all-out war as Serb forces intensified their raids on ethnic Albanians. Hundreds of thousands of residents were forced from their homes, thousands of them living in the woods without adequate clothing or shelter.

"There was daily news of massacres. You could hear explosions in Pristina. We got used to it. In the beginning of 1999 I saw some of my friends armed. I was with my cousin Zejna in Gjilan, and we helped internal refugees; we found them housing and food. Many Albanians opened their doors. There were soldiers everywhere. We watched them put mines in the streets. The regulars weren't bad; the reserves were bad," Zeqiri remembers. Meanwhile, a NATO deadline for Milosevic to come to terms on Kosovo or face bombing was approaching.

"On March 24, 1999, we saw the situation escalate. I took my wife and three kids, and my cousin took his wife and two kids, to a village called Miratoc on the border with Macedonia. We knew if they find my cousin and me, they will kill us." Zeqiri's plan was to send his family to a relative in Kumanova, an ethnic Albanian city in neighboring Macedonia, while his cousin and he would go back to fight. (Later that night, after people from Miratoc gathered 5,000 German marks and bribed the Macedonian border control to get them through, his family made it safely into Macedonia.) At 5:00 p.m., he went to his village to see his mother before he left to fight.

"My mom said, 'I know you're not going to tell me where you're going. But if you die, die like a man,'" Zeqiri recalls, explaining her injunction to him to fight as "our Albanian tradition." Zeqiri told his parents to take his sister, brother-in-law, and their two daughters to relatives in Presheva, where it was safer, while he and his brother stayed in Kokaj. His father left with them, but his mother said, "I can't leave you like this," and she stayed. That evening, NATO bombs fell.

"We had prepared in my cousin's house basement enough food for 100 people. Sadly, we had no weapons, but my cousin's father had a shotgun, which I kept," he says. "There were a lot of soldiers and explosions." Large numbers of refugees arrived at his house, where he had stored 1,000 kilos of flour and other materials to survive in the outdoors. For the next few days, there was heavy bombing, which the Albanians applauded, despite the danger, he says.

"On April 4, around 9:00 a.m., we heard shooting. I said to my mom, 'Soldiers are coming. I have to go to my uncle's house to tell him to go away.' I hugged her, she kissed me, and I said, 'It will be OK. Just go away. Don't think about me.' I went to my uncle, took his son Sevdail, who was fourteen years old, and told my uncle to go away. Then, about 200 feet behind me, I saw the soldiers. They tied my hands. I heard them say on the phone to their commandant, 'We found two guys, one looking like KLA, the other a child.'" Zeqiri could understand enough Serbo-Croatian to hear the reply—words he will never forget: "Kill immediately!"

One of the soldiers pushed Zeqiri to the ground, hit him on the back of the head with his gun, and shot at him. Bullets hit the ground all around him.

"I wasn't afraid. In those seconds, I thought about my family. I thought about my boy—I'm going to leave something behind," he says. It took him a few minutes before he realized he could move, that he hadn't been killed after all. However, what followed was an interrogation about KLA presence in the area that made him wish for a quick death.

A Serb paramilitary with bloodstained hands and his head wrapped in the characteristic bandana of the irregulars, put questions to him such as, "Which eye do you want out first? Which arm? Which leg?" To these questions, the prisoner answered, "Take them both. You're going to kill me anyway." His tormentor then ran his bayonet from Zeqiri's groin to his neck—but his leather jacket saved him, he believes. In the end, the soldiers and commandant let him go, apparently because he was unarmed and had convinced them that there were no KLA guerillas in the area. After taking his money, ID, car license, and other documents, they shoved him off with the warning, "Never come back here."

"As long as you're here, I'll never come back," he replied.

At the time of his arrest, Zeqiri lost some possessions almost as dear to him as his own life, confiscated during the raid on his house—his Albanian books and flag, as well as the manuscript of a book he had spent twelve years writing. Returning home to an empty house, he located his fourteen-year-old cousin, and the two walked to Presheva, surrounded by the sounds of gunfire.

"The shooting was normal now. I wasn't scared," he says. In Presheva, they joined Zeqiri's brother and another cousin and fled with them toward the Macedonian border, where a thousand other refugees were waiting to cross. Just before they reached the border, Serb soldiers and a drunken paramilitary separated the men from the women, and a paramilitary shot at Zeqiri's group, who dropped to the ground. Zeqiri remembers thinking it would be lucky for him to be killed quickly with a bullet. But once again, he escaped death when a Serb officer arrived on the scene and released him and his cousin.

At first, the Macedonians didn't let the refugees cross the border, so they had to stay in the mountains for a time in freezing cold, surrounded by snipers. More refugees flooded to the border. Among them was a relative of Zeqiri's who reported that many of his cousins had been killed. After bribing some Macedonians, he and his cousin crossed the border, where they discovered they were in a mine zone. They had had nothing to eat in two days. Finally, they got to Kumanova, where Zeqiri's wife and children had been waiting for two weeks, not knowing if he was alive or dead. There, he heard the heartbreaking news that paramilitaries had killed his mother as she fled her home soon after he had bid her good-bye.

The Zeqiri family's journey to America began soon afterward, in a Macedonian refugee camp called Camp Stenkovac, where they were assigned to Maine. In July 1999, they arrived in Portland, which Zeqiri praises as a "good, quiet" city with little crime. The Zeqiris, who are U.S. citizens, have prospered through hard work. Before he knew English, Zeqiri worked in a series of low-level jobs, beginning with his first, as a car cleaner and driver for companies. He now has a good job as a machine operator at Nichols Portland, an automotive parts manufacturer.

"It's not easy to do any job that was given to me here," says Zeqiri, because he can't use the hard-won university degree so highly prized in Kosovo. He had to sacrifice his goal of becoming a high-school teacher. "In future, maybe I'll do that—better late than never!" he says. "For now, I have to pay the mortgage." He and his wife, who works as a hotel housekeeper, own a home in Portland roomy enough for their family of six; in 2001, another son was born, in Portland. The couple intend to put their four children through college.

"I will be here with my family forever. I feel free and safe here," he says.

On a trip to Kosovo in 2004, Zeqiri was asked to take a teaching job, but declined. "When I visit the country, it's much more sad. Nobody is there in the villages. All the people left. When I'm there, I feel sick," he says. By most estimates, ethnic cleansing and warfare drove out some 800,000 Kosovars, the vast majority Albanians, to other countries. In the Kosovo-Serbian border region where Zeqiri lived, the houses were burned, and almost no jobs exist, he reports.

His own siblings and cousins scattered, some to Austria and Switzerland. Only his father remains in their home. Although they all talk by videophone weekly, Zeqiri misses them intensely. His consolation is the good life he has found in America. His free time is spent teaching his kids the Albanian language, seeing friends, and playing one of six musical instruments he has mastered—violin, clarinet, guitar, keyboard, drums, and *quifteli*, an Albanian two-stringed mandolin. Every November 28, he celebrates Flag Day—but not with the new flag created upon Kosovo's independence from Serbia in February 2008, which shows a map of Kosovo. That map could change any time, Zeqiri believes. Instead, he will continue to honor the red Albanian banner, relishing the freedom he now enjoys to display it.

RIFAT AND TASNEEM ZAIDI

As a young orthopedic surgeon, Rifat Zaidi wanted to work in public health in his native Pakistan. But, rather than welcoming his years of foreign training and specialized skills, the local medical establishment put up barriers. So he wound up going in a different direction—one that ultimately led him to Miles Memorial Hospital in the midcoast village of Damariscotta, where he has practiced orthopedics since 2002.

When a catastrophic earthquake struck Pakistan in October 2005, he knew he could help, since so many of the injuries involved broken bones. In just two weeks, he raised $30,000, rounded up donated medical equipment, and gathered a team from his hospital to accompany him to Pakistan. From his perch in a Maine village, he has since generated more support, conducted more medical missions to Pakistan, and helped found a burn center there.

Today, he sees the irony. "I'm doing more public service sitting here than I was doing there. I can afford to," he says.

Such daunting projects are doable in the universe of Rifat and his wife Tasneem, a physician herself who partners with him in the medical relief efforts. Settled comfortably with their two children in a serene small-town life in Newcastle, they have found a way to give back to the country that launched them in life.

Rifat was born in 1959 and raised in Lahore, Pakistan's second largest city after Karachi. His father was an eminent banker, author, and professor who was twice nominated for the King Faisal Award, the Arab world's equivalent of the Nobel Prize. As a government adviser, he pioneered the Islamization of Pakistan's banks to create an interest-free system based on distribution, rather than accumulation, of wealth, including zakat, or annual alms-giving of a portion of one's unused wealth. His mother wrote fiction and performed on a live weekly children's radio show.

Although his father was very busy, he always came home for dinner, at which time Rifat and his four siblings underwent a friendly interrogation as their father asked, "How much studying did you do today?" Luckily, Rifat was a good student at his English-language public school. A sickly child prone to allergies, he made frequent visits to doctor's offices, although he doesn't believe that figured into his decision to become a doctor. Educated Pakistani families encouraged their children to go into professional careers such as medicine, engineering, the military, or civil service for the prestige and financial security they offered.

"I always wanted to be a physician, and I happened to have enough grades to get to the next level. I was never an all-A student. I made the right side of the cut every time—there was a lot of element of luck," laughs Rifat, who never let studies edge out his cricket-playing, even at Rawalpindi Medical College.

A cosmopolitan city of 3 million people in the Punjab, Rawalpindi was Pakistan's capital before nearby Islamabad was built in the 1960s, and Pakistan's armed forces are still based there. Tasneem, whose father was an army officer, would later meet Rifat there, and the "twin cities" would figure heavily in their life together. Although she no longer practices medicine, she too trained as a physician—no surprise, in her family. "All the girls went to medical school. Most of my aunts and cousins became doctors. I just drifted into it," she says.

Tasneem's family are Pukhtuns (also called Pashtuns or Pathans). Large landowners from the North-West Frontier Province near the Afghanistan border, their fortunes fell briefly after a British agent assassinated her grandfather, Hayat Khan, for anti-Raj activities, and his lands were confiscated. Fortunately, his father-in-law bought the land back and transferred it to Tasneem's father.

Although Pukhtun tribal codes for women are ultraconservative in the province's remote mountainous regions, Pukhtuns in its settled areas believe in educating girls, and families like Tasneem's that can afford it have traditionally sent their daughters to elite British schools and colleges. Women in her family were educated—her mother finished high school and later regretted not going to medical school, and Tasneem attended boarding school in Murree Hill Station, a Punjabi resort area in the Himalayan foothills, from the age of seven.

She graduated from Khyber Medical College in Peshawar and did a cardiology residency, but gave up medicine once she and Rifat were married and starting a family, as he was moving from place to place in his own medical training.

After graduating from medical college in 1984 and training at Rawalpindi General Hospital, Rifat sought further training abroad.

"I wanted to come to America to get training in orthopedics. I actually never wanted to live in America," he says. Although he passed the American equivalence exam, it was hard to get a residency in the U.S. at the time, so he went to the United Kingdom instead. After taking professional qualifying exams in Scotland, he had an initial unpleasant training experience in a town in the south of England where he found the people snobbish and racially discriminatory. Then he headed as far north as he could, winding up for three years in Carlisle, a Lake District city. There he found warmhearted people appreciative of his surgical care, and ample scope for his cricket-playing.

As that training came to an end in 1992, a call came from his father in Rawalpindi: "Come home. You're getting married." Since Rifat, who was in his early thirties, never said no to his father, home he went, and he spent the next two months undergoing what Rifat calls "girl viewing," the process of looking over potential brides in family get-togethers.

"My parents had short-listed three girls. Tasneem was one of the finalists, though we don't speak the same language [his first language was Urdu, hers was Pashto]. Our houses were a few miles from each other, and our parents knew each other," he says. When visits with the initial contenders didn't turn up a winner, Rifat said, "Let's keep looking." Then his family all went to Tasneem's parents' home.

"This is good," Rifat pronounced after meeting Tasneem, who liked what she saw, too.

"I had told my parents I wasn't interested in any Pukhtun guys; they're a little bit conservative. I had informed my mother that if I were to go for an arranged marriage, short-listed candidates should be physicians like me and non-Pukhtuns. I fell for him as soon as I saw him," she says, impressed with his looks, intelligence, and sense of humor.

"I was working at the hospital. He came to see me there, and we talked till 2:00 a.m." The next day they met for lunch, after ditching her chaperoning sister. Three months later, they married in a five-day wedding that cemented the alliance between the two families. The whole heady process amounted to what Rifat calls a "hybrid"—an arranged marriage where both parties got to choose among finalists.

"It actually works better, because the background is all taken care of for you by the parents," says Tasneem.

"You have been pre-approved," adds Rifat.

The young couple moved to England, where Rifat continued his training at various hospitals in the north for a few years until an offer came for a clinical fellowship in pediatric orthopedics at Children's Hospital of Buffalo in New York. They enjoyed their year in Buffalo, regularly visiting Niagara Falls like other newlyweds, then returned to northern England, to a hospital in Darlington. By the time they left the U.K. in 1996, they had two children—their daughter Izza and their son Syed Osama ("Syed" is an honorific title denoting lineage from the Prophet Muhammad's family). They decided to return to their homeland.

"I never had the ambition to stay abroad. I wanted to go back and set up practice. That's our country," says Rifat. His father had passed away, leaving his mother alone in Rawalpindi. A year earlier, Tasneem's mother had been murdered in a burglary at her home, and Tasneem was the eldest child in her close-knit family. In addition, Rifat didn't want to be part of Pakistan's brain drain. "A lot of us come over and never go back and offer anything to the country," he says. (Rifat isn't the only "international" person in his family. His four siblings live on four different continents—one brother is a UN peacekeeper in Congo, another works for UNICEF in Geneva, a third is an architect in Islamabad, and his sister lives in Dubai, where her husband is a banker.)

Once the Zaidis were settled in Rawalpindi and Rifat was practicing at an Islamabad hospital, an offer came through that he couldn't refuse—a fellowship in the unique orthopedic subspecialty of limb lengthening and reconstruction surgery at the University of Maryland hospital in Baltimore, the only fellowship of its kind in North America. So he left his family for six months, after which he returned to Rawalpindi for good—or so he thought.

For the next six years, he worked in Islamabad as a consulting orthopedic surgeon at Shifa International Hospital, a new, state-of-the-art private facility where all the consultant staff are trained abroad. He also taught at its affiliated College of Medicine, where he remains on the faculty as a visiting physician.

There was just one problem: not enough patients could afford to use his highly specialized services. Yet when he applied for posts in the public system at children's hospitals in Lahore and Islamabad, he was told he was not qualified.

"They didn't want a trained person to come and take away their practice," he says. Nepotism in such public hospitals was also a major hurdle. At Shifa, he never refused surgery to a patient who couldn't pay, and it worried him that without enough paying patients, he might never be able to send his children to college. Meanwhile, Pakistan's mounting political turmoil, 1998 nuclear tests, armed robberies, and kidnappings were causing his wife and him serious concern. Rifat slept with a gun next to his bed, and they tried to keep a low profile by driving an inexpensive car and not improving the outside of their house.

"So that euphoria of patriotism started to evaporate," he says. Furthermore, his thirteen-hour workdays and long commute were getting to him. Then, one day in August 2001, a torrential rainfall funneled down from the Himalayas and flooded his hospital, destroying all essential hospital services, his car and his job, and he finally had enough. "I think, this is God's push, telling me to move on," he recalls.

With that, Tasneem got on the Internet and researched American locations. In their Buffalo days, they had visited Maine and liked the state, one of only a handful accepting British training. They knew they wanted a quiet setting, rather than a big city.

"Let's go to Maine," they decided. But that wasn't so simple. An interview that was set up in Geneva, Switzerland, with a doctor from Miles Memorial Hospital in Damariscotta got canceled, so Rifat headed to England for a quick visit with a friend before his planned flight to Damariscotta. Suddenly the September 11 attacks struck, canceling flights and leaving him stranded in England for three months, jobless. He tried to find work there, without luck.

"Because of being a Pakistani and a Muslim, I'm not getting anywhere. Pakistan was implicated in 9/11," he says. Finally, he landed a short-term stint in Wales. The hospital in the town of Merthyr Tydfil was desperate for an orthopedic surgeon. "I'm desperate, too," he told them. Eventually, he was able to fly home to Pakistan to get his visa stamped.

People there were still in shock over 9/11. "Cruise missiles were flying over Pakistan to Afghanistan. Things were tense," Tasneem remembers.

In April 2002, they were relieved to arrive in the U.S. with their children and settle into Newcastle-Damariscotta on the Damariscotta River, one of Maine's most scenic coastal areas. Rifat's wish for a better balance between work and home life came true—until the next upheaval, in a life by now filled with intercontinental crossings. In October 2005, a devastating earthquake hit northern Pakistan and Kashmir, killing more than 80,000 people and leaving millions homeless. "I said, 'I need to go back,'" says Rifat, who started calling his contacts in Pakistan. "That's where my five years working in Pakistan helped me." Tasneem handled administrative duties, and together they mobilized local support in short order, raising $30,000 and acquiring a quarter of a million dollars' worth of donated medical equipment. Rifat led a medical mission that included two doctors and two nurses from Miles Memorial Hospital. They operated on patients with broken bones in an Islamabad hospital, as well as in the field up north. Tasneem's and his families opened their homes and offered other assistance to the volunteers.

Since then, Rifat has led follow-up surgical missions. Discovering the need for a burn center, he raised another $30,000 and created one in basement space at his alma mater, Rawalpindi Medical College—a four-bed center whose plastic surgeons are paid through the Rawalpindi Medical College Overseas Foundation he helped found. He is also trying to buy a piece of land for a surgery center. Every year, he returns to Pakistan and operates on patients free of charge. At last, he is able to perform the public service he wanted to do as a young doctor.

To generate funds for the quake-relief and burn-center efforts, Tasneem, who holds an M.B.A., has started a "business aid" web store, www.traditionsonweb.com, to sell fine handicrafts from the earthquake-affected regions of Kashmir and northern Pakistan.

A family life with deep connections in both Maine and Pakistan seems to work out gracefully for the Zaidis. They find no problem in living in a place where Pakistanis are scarce. Nor is the lack of a mosque an impediment. "We pray at home, observe Ramazan, pay zakat (giving a percentage of one's income to charity), and don't eat non-halal products. We're just like regular people," Rifat says, practicing their faith as one part of their lives and engaging in other activities the rest of the time. In summertime, those activities include golf, swimming, tennis, kayaking, and soccer, as well as horseback riding and sailing lessons for their children. Once a year, the family travels from the "twin villages" of Damariscotta-Newcastle to the "twin cities" of Rawalpindi-Islamabad.

Rifat is glad that his son and daughter spent five years of their early lives in Pakistan, where they got to know the culture and their extended families. Both children are keen to become physicians, too. "Being a physician is a good job. You have a lot of respect," Rifat tells them. Balancing his career with a rich family life and giving back to the country that raised him reflects his healthy predilection for "other things to do in life" besides work. If only one of those other things included cricket playing in Maine.

"There's a conspiracy there," he laughs.

Note: Donations to the earthquake and burn center funds may be made by check to Dr. Rifat Zaidi, indicating at the bottom of the check "Medical Relief Fund" and/or "Burn Centre," and sent to: Dr. Rifat Zaidi, Salt Bay Orthopaedics, Miles Memorial Hospital, Bristol Road, Damariscotta, ME 04543

WINSTON WILLIAMS

Most people shopping for quality produce at the popular Beth's Farm Market never meet Winston Williams. Yet he is indispensable to it. As foreman of a sixteen-man crew of seasonal workers at White Oak Farms in Warren, a midcoast Maine town, he is responsible for making sure those crops grow and get harvested correctly and on time.

Williams has been an integral part of Maine life since first coming to the state almost twenty years ago. He lives here for most of the year, working behind the scenes to produce vegetables and fruit on which local consumers and several New England restaurants and food companies depend. It isn't until the snow starts to fly in November or December that he goes home to Jamaica, to his other life. There he has a wife and three children whom he only sees for a few months before returning to Maine in March and starting the growing cycle all over again.

After almost two decades of working at the same farm, Williams has developed a close relationship with its owners, Vincent and Beth Ahlholm, who have visited his family in Jamaica. Half of the farm's all-Jamaican crew is from Williams's own town, having heard about the job through word of mouth. The workers are attracted mainly by the good wage, $9.70 an hour at this writing. Williams says they can earn up to $500 or $600 a week, more than they can make picking apples or cutting sugar cane—two jobs he and many other Jamaicans have also done.

"There's more money here than sugar cane and apples. It make life better for me. I build my own house, buy a new car," says Williams, speaking in a lilting Jamaican English colored with Jamaican patois, the dialect many Jamaicans use informally. "It's very hard to get a job in Jamaica. Also, when you go out and work, you learn about other people's cultures," he says.

On the farm, Williams lives by himself in a trailer, with the tractors he drives parked outside. Across the road, behind the farm market, the farm workers live in two bunkhouses near the farmhouse and outbuildings. They all put in long hours in the fields—sometimes up to sixty hours a week, depending on the weather and time of year.

"I take orders from Vince and pass it on. I see that the work done the right way, where to go, what to pick," says Williams. Since most of the men have worked together for years, very few problems emerge, and if they do, they are quickly sorted out.

"We are united together; it make things go easy," he says.

At the end of the day, the workers relax in the bunkhouse, sometimes playing dominoes.

When they have time off, they go shopping in Augusta or Lewiston, or visit fairs in the area. Williams is usually so tired after driving the tractor all day that he prefers to relax in his trailer alone and read or watch TV most evenings.

"I don't like too much crowds," he says. Williams, a diabetic, usually cooks for himself, keeping to a healthy diet of lots of vegetables from the farm. That diet and the good exercise he gets at work help keep his diabetes under control, he believes. Every day, he connects by cell phone with his family in Jamaica, using calling cards. When it is cold in Maine, his family jokes with him, "It's warm down here. Why don't you come down here?" He sends money regularly by Western Union to his wife, who also worked seasonally in the U.S., at hotels in Michigan and Florida for four years, but now is busy at home.

Williams has two grown children, a daughter who is a homemaker and a son who recently switched from auto mechanics to carpentry and is helping Williams build a house. He also has a daughter who is still in high school. Over the years, when his children were young, he found it hard to leave them.

"Sure, I miss them. When it's time for me to leave, they cry, I cry," he says. But he would explain to them that he was working for a better life for the family, and that he would always come back.

Free time at White Oak Farms includes occasional cookouts featuring a stew of curried goat meat and rice, a Jamaican favorite. At other times, Williams shares dinner with the Ahlholms, whom he calls "very good people." Vincent Ahlholm runs the 400-acre growing operation, some of which spreads over leased fields. His wife Beth teaches in a local school and works at the extensive farm market, a store that began as a small roadside stand two decades ago and now overflows with tomatoes, greens, strawberries, Maine blueberries, apples, melons, homemade baked goods and preserves, flowers, and nursery plants. The respect Williams expresses for his employers is mutual; Beth says they feel extremely lucky to have had Williams working at the farm for so many years.

When Williams first came to the farm in 1990, he was already a seasoned worker from previous temporary jobs in the U.S. Following in his parents' footsteps, he had left his country because he couldn't find well-paying work at home. He was born in 1957 in May Pen, a small city in southern Jamaica that is the capital of the populous Clarendon Parish, notable as the birthplace of several top reggae singers, including Toots Hibbert of Toots and the Maytals, as well as world champion boxer Glen Johnson. Because of poverty, hundreds of thousands of Jamaicans have emigrated from the tropical island nation just south of Cuba or, like Williams, migrated seasonally to other countries for work.

"I grew up with my grandparents because my mother leave to England when I was one and a half. My father leave before her for England. They leave to improve themselves. With our culture, the grandparents love to raise the kids," says Williams, who called his grandparents Mom and Dad growing up. His parents worked in British factories and sent money on holidays to the brick home in Clarendon where Williams lived as the man of the house until he was in his late twenties.

"My grandparents take very good care of me, treat me like a king," says Williams, who got lots of attention as the only child. He started helping out on the five-acre family farm of sugar cane, coffee, and chocolate when he was six years old. By the time he was ten, he was farming like an adult, missing a few weeks of school each year during the cane harvest.

For fun, he and his friends played cricket and soccer, or went fishing in the river running through the wide plain of the parish, or hung out on the nearby beach on the Caribbean Sea. At school, he played on the cricket and volleyball teams. He liked all the school subjects, and at home he obeyed the strict rule of his grandmother when it was time to do homework: "No playing. It's book time." He credits his grandparents with teaching him to value intelligence, good behavior, good manners, and discipline.

"My grandmom was a Christian lady," says Williams, who accompanied her to the New Testament Church of God, which he describes as "one of the loud ones where we shout 'Hallelulah.'" Religion didn't get in the way of his partying and dancing to reggae music when he got older, however. "I loved reggae music like Bob Marley," he says.

In 1975, when his grandfather died, Williams's mother returned to Jamaica for a visit—the first time the eighteen-year-old Winston had seen her since he was a baby. "It was very rough" emotionally, he says. Until then, he had only known her through letters and photographs sent from England. From then on, she visited more often.

After ninth grade, Williams learned auto mechanics by working at an auto-repair garage. He then worked as a public minibus driver for three years before hearing about a program bringing Jamaican workers to the U.S. under temporary agricultural-labor visas. After passing a medical exam, he was accepted and left his country in 1986 to work cutting sugar cane for a sugar company in Florida from November to April.

"It was very hard for me. Chopping sugar cane is hard work, and it was real hot," he recalls. He missed his family, and in those pre–cell phone days, they had to rely on letters back and forth.

In Florida, someone told him that picking apples was much easier work, so for the next three years, he picked apples in New York's Hudson Valley, returning to the same farm each year. Although he earned less than he had cutting sugar cane, the work was not as grueling.

"You earn enough to support your family, pay your bills and save a little," he recalls. Then he heard about White Oak Farms from his father-in-law, who had worked there and recommended Williams to Ahlholm. In 1990 Williams started work at the farm, and four years later he was promoted to foreman.

Williams says he and his fellow Jamaicans have had a good experience in Maine. Although the town of Warren is 97 percent white, he can only remember one time when someone shouted a racist remark at them from a car, and no one has ever accused the migrant workers of taking away local jobs. "We never heard of anyone saying, 'Don't work here,'" he says. In fact, growers in Maine, as in other states, cannot find enough local workers to do the backbreaking labor, and not only at vegetable farms. Hundreds of Jamaicans also make up the bulk of the apple-picking work force in Maine, under the same temporary agricultural worker, or federal H-2A, program that brings Williams and his fellow farm workers to Maine each year.

"I like Maine. Peoples very friendly, not a lot of crime—that's what the guys like here. The only problem we have with Maine is the cold," he says.

Back home in Jamaica, Williams used to keep on working through the winter, driving a taxi, until a few years ago. As he grows older, he dreams of cutting back to fewer months spent in Maine each year "to make it easier for me and for my family," he says. "I hope someday things will be better and I can stay longer with my family. God do a lot of things for me, so I trust Him."

SUWANNA SANGUANTONKALLAYA

As a child in Thailand, Suwanna Sanguantonkallaya proved herself capable of doing man's work on her family's farm. She had a goal of owning her own business someday, even though that didn't fit the role society outlined for women in her culture. While she tried her hand at a few business ventures early on, it wasn't until she opened her first restaurant in Portland that she came into her own. Now, fourteen years after arriving in Maine, she has opened her third eatery.

"They give me a new life here in America. You can dream from here. A woman can do business by herself. In Thailand, they believe only men can do everything," she says.

Suwanna owns Sengchai Thai Cuisine on Forest Avenue, and she recently launched Thai Chef Buffet on downtown Congress Street with a mission to offer a new kind of heart-healthy, low-fat Thai cooking, a cuisine already noted for its tasty lightness. In a city with at least a half-dozen Thai restaurants, she has held her own and expanded. But the road to her current success has not been easy.

Born in 1959 in Khon Kaen, a city in the northeastern part of Thailand near Laos, Suwanna was the fourth of nine children. Her parents were large landowners who raised pigs and chickens and employed up to thirty farm workers. Not only did Suwanna help with farming, she also cooked often for the family from the time she was nine years old.

"You need to know everything," her mother told her. "That way when you have a husband, they will know you come from a good family." She was taught to keep the house spotless and smelling good, because that's what men liked at home. "She was very old-fashioned," says Suwanna, who had a rebellious streak and got spanked by her mother sometimes, which didn't stop her from indulging in unladylike activities such as boxing. "I was a strong girl," she says.

She admired her father, an educated man whose employees called him "Daddy" because he treated them well, "like I treat my employees," she adds. He not only oversaw the business, but also played the violin, inspiring Suwanna to play the guitar and pursue her love of Thai dancing and singing.

The family was close, and enjoyed regular potluck dinners with their many relatives. With a Vietnamese-Thai mother and a Chinese-Thai father, the children spoke both Vietnamese and Chinese at home, although at school they spoke Thai. Suwanna lived at home, working on the farm, long after she finished school in ninth grade, when her mother told her that women didn't need to learn much because they could just get married. Suwanna, who had been an excellent student, had higher aspirations, partly drawn from her constant reading. One day she was enthralled to read about Neil Armstrong landing on the moon.

"Daddy, how can people go to the moon?" she asked her father. He replied, "These people in America are very smart," and at that moment her dream of visiting the U.S. was born.

Suwanna wanted to own her own business, like her father, and make good money. She didn't think much about marriage. But when she was twenty, her mother found a husband for her, after a search based on two main criteria Suwanna recalls as "no gamble, be healthy." She could not say no, out of respect for her parents. "I must do," she says, although she doesn't remember feeling one way or the other about it. Luckily, it turned out to be an excellent match, since her husband was not only a good man, but also rich, with a thriving construction business. In 1979, they married.

For a time, the business went well, with Suwanna sharing the load as well as operating her own building-supply store out of their home in Nam Phong, site of an air base used by the U.S. military during the Vietnam War. Eventually, though, the bribery demands of corrupt government inspectors dragged them down financially, entangled them in court cases whose outcomes changed with the changing politics, and wound up bankrupting them. The couple tried out Suwanna's dream of coming to America in 1988, visiting Los Angeles, where they had family, for a few months, but returning to Thailand when her husband decided he didn't want to live in the U.S. For the next two years, the financial strain continued as they depended on his sister for support; by then they had two young sons, and no relief in sight from money worries.

Suwanna decided to return to the U.S. on her own to try her luck. "I'm independent," she says. She had a cousin in Maryland urging her to come because of a good U.S. business climate. She worked for a while in a fishhook manufacturing and sales venture, traveling to Minnesota and Maine for their recreational fishing markets. She remembered reading about the White Mountains and Bar Harbor when she was young, and heard that Maine had a lot of lakes. When that venture failed, she found herself in Portland in 1994, turning to a different skill she knew she had: cooking. She got hired at a local Asian restaurant, where she eventually became a business partner.

Promising herself that she would make money, Suwanna opened her own restaurant, Seng Thai Cuisine on St. John Street in Portland, and soon became very busy. The restaurant was thriving on its strong word-of-mouth reputation, when one day in February 2001, calamity struck. A fire started in the basement and destroyed the restaurant; its cause was never determined, she says. Tragically, a Thai waitress, a good friend of Suwanna's, died in the fire. Devastated emotionally and financially, Suwanna returned home to Thailand to recover.

"It made me crazy," she says. After six months—a time filled with meditation and nurturing family support—she returned to Portland, determined to try another restaurant.

Sengchai Thai Cuisine, which opened on Forest Avenue in 2003, is the result. Today, her teenaged daughter works there when she isn't in class at the private Waynflete School in Portland. Proud that her daughter can handle whatever happens at the restaurant, Suwanna thinks it is important for her to learn what she can by working in the family business.

"It's the Asian way, to work with families," she says. By now her sons are in their twenties and working in their own professions in Thailand; one is a civil engineer, and the other is completing medical school.

Sadly, just eight months after the fire, Suwanna's husband died of a heart attack, rocking her emotionally once again. With advice from her medical-student son, she has studied the connection between a low-fat diet and preventing heart disease. She is putting what she has learned to use in her latest venture, Thai Chef Buffet, where the emphasis is on good nutrition. In Thailand, too, people are becoming more health-conscious, she says, citing her mother's exercise program at the age of eighty-four.

"All the people exercise. Our own king, too," she says, referring to King Bhumibol Adulyadej, one of the longest-reigning monarchs in history. Thailand is a constitutional monarchy that was known as Siam until 1939. Although it borders Laos and Cambodia in a region devastated by the Vietnam War and Khmer Rouge regime during Suwanna's youth, Thailand was never colonized by a Western power and remained relatively calm in modern times as it seesawed between military dictatorship and democratic regimes. The capital, Bangkok, is Southeast Asia's financial center, although the country still holds a reputation for corruption, as Suwanna found out in her construction-business days.

Today, having overcome setbacks that might have knocked out a less determined person long ago, she has learned how to succeed in business by trying—very hard, again and again. In 2005, she won a Businesswoman of the Year Award and traveled to Washington, D.C., to receive it in a ceremony attended by President Bush.

Unfazed by putting in long hours every day, seven days a week, at her two restaurants, Suwanna looks back with satisfaction on having made her childhood dream come true. As a mother, she is proud of her daughter's skills and the achievements of her civil engineer and doctor sons—all of them hard workers like herself.

"When my husband died, I knew I needed to take care of everything, so I work seven days a week. When you see your sons and daughter do good, you're not tired," she says.

Rafael Galvez

"It's not just another IMMIGRATION case. It's your FUTURE," reads the heading on the website of a low-key lawyer not given to hyperbole so much as dedication to a cause. One of only a handful of foreign-born lawyers in Maine, Peruvian Rafael Galvez knows on a personal level how challenging it is to make it in a foreign land.

On a professional level, since opening his Portland practice several years ago, he has learned what perseverance it takes for immigrants to overcome barriers to reuniting with their loved ones or becoming U.S. citizens. Along the way, Galvez has formed a commitment to fighting for a compassionate, fair immigration system. He has organized rallies and spoken out publicly against hostility toward undocumented immigrants and attempts to restrict citizenship.

"That's where my heart is—in immigration policy. It's my passion," he says. At a time of mounting deportations of undocumented workers and workers returning voluntarily to their native countries because they fear arrest and deportation, Galvez urges legal and social acceptance of deserving undocumented immigrants and recognition that if laws aren't changed, American families will continue to suffer from separation caused by deportations.

"It is not enough for the legal system to bring the undocumented out of the shadows of society; society itself must accept that, like most people, undocumented immigrants come to the U.S. to work hard for a better future," he says.

Galvez has come a long way from a shy childhood in a working-class family in Lima. Although both his parents held professional degrees, success in his impoverished nation was difficult to attain. The Peru of his childhood in the 1980s was economically turbulent, with high inflation and rising drug trafficking. From the mid-1980s, armed conflict between the Maoist Shining Path guerrillas and government forces escalated, resulting in bombings, killings, and disappearances across Peru's countryside.

"I was lucky to feel safe, because the violence had not reached explosive levels where I lived," says Galvez, who remembers blackouts and hearing about the violence and national strikes in news programs and family discussions. "You get used to hearing the news. It becomes part of life."

Looking back on it, Galvez identifies the factors resulting in the powder keg of 1980s Peru as corruption, inept leaders, lack of infrastructure, and economic instability evident in unemployment and underemployment. Contributing to the volatile combination was visible inequality. "Peruvians of lighter *mestizo* [mixed Amerindian and Spanish] complexion tended to economically and socially dominate their indigenous countrymen," he says. By the late 1980s, the situation became untenable for his family.

"Food was becoming scarce. You had to wait hours in line to buy basic food staples," he says. Political violence was spreading, and economic instability led to the absence of real-life opportunities to the point where professionals were driving taxis to eke out a living. One day soon after Galvez turned thirteen, his mother told her two children that they would soon be leaving for the U.S.

"My mother did not see a decent future for her children; my parents had also split up earlier. She warned my sister and me that we may have to struggle at the beginning." Galvez praises her wisdom in presenting a realistic picture to his sister and him, rather than projecting a false sense of optimism. Along with his mother and sister, Galvez joined an aunt and uncle in South Florida who helped his family settle into their new homeland.

"Life was good. I had nothing to worry about except for going to school, helping my mother in her cleaning job, and writing checks for her in English," he says. The family started with little in their new life. "We had no reason to complain," says Galvez. His mother, who spoke very little English, frequently held two janitorial jobs at the same time. For a former teacher, the low-level work must have been frustrating, but Galvez didn't detect disappointment. "We recognized that we had to start from the bottom and work our way up," he says.

He quickly abandoned his heritage with the same effervescence he brought to learning English and blending in in his new home. "I quickly forgot where I came from. That's truly regretful," admits Galvez, who lost touch with his relatives in Peru. He also regrets not doing better in high school. Although he performed well academically, neither he nor his teachers recognized that he could enroll in challenging courses. "I was very far behind from what I could accomplish. In my last semester of high school, people began to ask, 'Where are you going to college?' It wasn't part of my vocabulary. I was oblivious to all that."

Then one day, borrowing a classmate's career objective, he realized he wanted to become a lawyer. After graduating from high school, Galvez attended a local community college. Soon his curiosity about New England led him to the University of Maine, where he studied political science. He immediately went on to law school at the University of Maine School of Law in Portland and, for the first time in his life, he had to break a sweat academically.

"Law school was boot camp for life. It's like rocket science and forces many students to doubt their intellectual abilities," says Galvez. "It was very tough, but I wouldn't give up after having this aspiration for so long." His hard work paid off upon graduating from law school and passing both the Maine and Massachusetts bar exams.

Galvez's achievements soon turned sour, however, as he faced the challenge of a post-9/11 economy and bleak job market. Since arriving as a teen in the U.S., he had not yet legally become an American. His peers in school had always assumed that he had no immigration problems since he had been in America so long. However, his road to legal security was a long one, typical of the kinds of difficulties encountered by his clients.

Galvez hadn't worried about his immigration status, thinking that eventually he would be able to become a U.S. citizen. While his mother gained her U.S. citizenship in the 1990s, Galvez was then too old to derive an immediate immigration benefit from her. He would have to wait much longer to receive permanent residence. He had not prepared for the reality that he would not have a green card by the time he passed the bar exam, so he spent years unable to work legally—a dilemma with life-changing implications.

"I was miserable," he says. "Here was a lawyer who could not find a solution to his own legal problem. I began to intensively study immigration law, to no avail. I had gotten ready to fly for so long, but I had no wings." As he worked at various legal and nonlegal jobs while he waited for his green card, he realized that his own struggle provided him the tools to navigate the rough seas of immigration law. "I received my permanent residence after fifteen years of living in the U.S. I had spent more than half my life in the U.S. before I could apply," he says. Once he got his green card in 2004, he decided to focus his career on immigration law.

Whether or not Maine is welcoming to immigrants "depends on the eyes of the beholder," says Galvez. "Protectionists will argue that Maine extends sanctuary to illegal immigrants. Progressives will charge that certain state and local agencies are providing a doorway for enforcement by federal officials—for example, police asking about immigration status when stopping motorists or pedestrians." On the surface, Maine is welcoming, and he feels personally welcome, but there are always hidden agendas, he says.

"Socially, the welcome mat to immigrants is very small. Many people incorrectly assume an undocumented person is a criminal who has to be deported because they have no rights. But people don't risk their lives through dangerous border deserts and hazardous voyages to become criminals. If the critic realized what the immigrant left behind, he might recognize the same experience his own predecessors experienced—leaving their countries and arriving penniless. For some reason, their Ellis Island is cherished, whereas today it is different. The legal avenues don't readily exist today, hence you have illegal immigration," he says.

Galvez has made it his personal cause to fight for immigration-law reform.

"It saddens me when I tell people that there is nothing the law can do for them, even when humanitarian equities are taken into consideration. It equally saddens me when deportation is proposed as a panacea. Mass deportations mean that families will be torn up," he says, adding that under the current immigration system parents and children often must remain separated from one another for more than five years before being reunited. "Coming to the U.S. legally is not as simple as 'applying for a visa' because those visas do not readily exist. In the absence of a legal avenue to enter the U.S., workers and families are compelled to enter illegally."

Galvez points out that the U.S. Supreme Court recognizes interstate travel as a fundamental right deserving the highest protection. "Yet Americans often do not realize that immigrants migrate for the same reasons that Americans move across state lines: seeking better economic opportunities, being closer to family, and fleeing disasters."

Would he ever return to Peru to live? "I wouldn't discard it as a possibility," he says, considering the close connections with his extended family that he has worked hard to reestablish. As for his Peruvian roots, he says, "I'm proud of my roots. If I have time, I'd like to regain them."

Based on what he has learned from years of formal education, practical legal experience, activism, and his own success as an immigrant from a poor country, he expresses optimism that America's immigration laws can change.

"If we can go to another planet, we should be able to do this," he says.

JADEN LI EUNG

First there was the whiteness of the population. Then there were the comments: "Gook!" and "Chink!"—words she had never heard before, despite having lived in rough, gang-ridden neighborhoods in different parts of the country. Although she was a tough twelve-year-old, Jaden Li Eung was deeply hurt by her unfriendly reception when she arrived in Maine in 1993.

"It was heartbreaking. I never felt like such an outsider. I was very angry. It was like being an immigrant all over again," says Eung, who had already lived in the U.S. for four years after her family fled war-torn Cambodia.

Today, Eung feels differently about Maine. In a Portland grown much more diverse, she found advantages as a college student in a small environment where she could make her mark. At the University of Southern Maine, she turned the pain of her immigrant experience into activism as founder of the campus's first Asian Association & Symposium, a member of the student senate, and an advocate for homeless youth. Once on the verge of homelessness herself, she now expresses a driving determination to help others going through what she went through during the years her family chased, but failed to capture, the American dream.

To be a young immigrant is to live a dichotomous life, pulled between a social world one tries hard to fit into and a traditional home life under stress from culture shock and economic strain. Like many immigrant children whose English language skills quickly surpass their parents', Eung was thrust into a demanding role as bridge to the new culture and head of household, raising her younger siblings while her parents worked long hours. In the process, she feels she lost her own childhood, which started out happily enough in Cambodia's northwest province of Battambang.

When Eung was born in 1981, the People's Republic of Kampuchea, as the country was known then, lay in ruins following the fall of the Khmer Rouge. Large numbers of refugees were still fleeing to camps in neighboring Thailand. Her family had lost everything, including their former prestige. Educated people such as her parents—her father was a French teacher and musician, her mother had completed middle school—had been purged. Her family lived in poverty, lacking even shoes to wear. Eung's earliest memory is of escaping to a Thai refugee camp when she was about six, with her parents, younger brother and sister, and several relatives.

"Our family was always on the run, digging in trenches, hiding in caves, running away from danger," recalls Eung, whose bare feet padded along the muddy, claylike earth, sometimes getting cut. They finally arrived at Khao I Dang, the sprawling United Nations refugee camp of some 140,000 Cambodians featured in the movie *The Killing Fields*. There, her family lived in a one-room bamboo hut with a dirt floor for about a year. While her parents worked in a sugar-cane field, Eung attended school and made her fun, especially delighting in playing in the rain.

"I was carefree in the camp. Life for me seemed happy," she says. But periodic raids by Khmer Rouge remnants drove their entire camp village to a large trench where they would hide for several hours. "I would hear bullets. I'd look at the sky and see long neon bullets like fireworks. The huts were ransacked when we went back."

After a brief stay in a different Thai refugee camp, the family was sent to the Philippines, where they lived in a transition camp for a year while being processed as refugees. Eung attended a school where classes were taught in English, ate her first hot dog, and saw her first movie, *Superman*. "I didn't understand it at all, but I loved it," she remembers. "I wanted to be just like him, flying around in the sky.

"My childhood ended there," she says.

Eung's family was sent to Memphis, where an uncle lived, and Eung took on the role of raising her siblings while her parents took English language classes, searched for work, and became involved in the Catholic Church, which had sponsored them to come to America. She struggled to adapt to living under a real roof, overcome her fear of using a flush toilet, and face school cafeteria food that made her gag. She was puzzled by the piles of presents arriving from strangers that first Christmas; she had never had toys before.

Before long, the family began a nomadic, increasingly unstable life, moving first to Norwalk, California, to live briefly with Eung's mother's relatives, and then to Long Beach, with its more generous welfare. By this time in the late 1980s, the "gangsta" era had arrived in Los Angeles County, with its large populations of poor Latinos, Asians, and blacks. Eung remembers being frightened walking to her elementary school through their ghetto, and sometimes saw guns fired. She was put in second grade, with a Spanish-speaking teacher, and Spanish became her second language, rather than English. After a switch to a school with more diversity, she made friends with other Cambodians conversing in Khmer, but also found English-speaking friends.

"I had to communicate, so I learned English," she says. Although her father could read English from his former teaching days in Cambodia, her parents were too busy scrambling for work to improve their language skills. She translated school letters for them and signed permission slips in their names. At first, her father helped his wife at home in her piecework sewing job. Sometimes they worked in a factory and were gone a lot. At eight years old, Eung walked home past gang members and let herself in with her own house key. No one was happy. Hope lay in a move to Joliet, Illinois, where a Cambodian friend of her father's lived.

"I was the only Asian in class. It was the true test of my being independent," says Eung.

She surged ahead academically, bringing home As, while her parents constantly searched for work—at times sewing or assembling rope products in their basement, and at other times working in factories. Unable to get ahead, they soon moved again—this time to Lowell, Massachusetts, a mill town nicknamed "Little Cambodia," where her father had relatives.

Like her former schools, Eung's new one had a diverse student population, mostly Hispanic and Asian. Unlike most of those students, however, she was in a mainstream class as the only Asian. Because she and her sister were more proficient in English than many other immigrants, they seemed to other students like California "Valley Girls." But Lowell, like other cities they had left, proved dangerous. With gang violence and drug deals taking place right in front of her house, Eung wasn't allowed to go out. To make matters worse, when she was eleven, her parents separated, their arranged marriage never having worked very well. Needing support as a single parent, Eung's mother moved her children back to the Los Angeles area, where her relatives had become successful business owners and took them in. Instead of finding comfort there, though, Eung found shame and anger.

"My family is quite unfortunate from the two sides of the extended family—besides being the poorest," says Eung. Her mother's sisters and their family own a jewelry store and a bakery. Eung was painfully aware of the disparity between herself and her more affluent cousins. While they had cars and computers, she and her family were sharing one bedroom in their home. "My parents were separating; we were back living among family again. We might as well have been refugees." At the affluent school she attended, she hid her shame.

"I'm this immigrant Asian American, but I'll never let it show that I'm poor and taking care of my family. I felt very lonely. I'd have a mask on at school," says Eung. As the oldest child and a girl, Eung felt she had a "double whammy," expected to take care of the home front as well as achieve at school. When this refuge failed as all the previous ones had, her mother took her children back again across the country, to Maine. A friend of Eung's mother had come to Portland to escape Lowell's gang violence.

"A lot of Cambodians are always running away to a newfound land," says Eung, who by then had moved, on average, twice a year. With her mother and younger siblings, she arrived in the middle of a snowstorm to a cramped apartment in Portland shared by another single mother and her eight children. School was a disappointment, too; Eung was placed in an ESL track in middle school, and her sister was put in a similar class. She was appalled, since they both were excellent students with good English. Pressing their case and handling the paperwork herself, Eung got them both transferred to a different school. Along with racial insults like "gook" that she heard on the school bus or on the street, she resented that some people assumed from her appearance that she didn't know English, whereas she was actually an honors student with a fervent ambition to attend Harvard or Duke University and become a lawyer.

In high school, she excelled academically, although her chaotic home life was starting to oppress her. Her mother wasn't around much of the time, and when she was, they argued. Soon, she couldn't concentrate at school. Growing more troubled, Eung didn't know how to ask for help; nor did the Khmer culture encourage talking about one's feelings. By her junior year, she started missing school, letting her grades fall, and partying. Years of playing an adult role had caught up with her.

"I just wanted to be a kid. I started questioning things, I discovered boys and started wanting to hang out and chill," she says. At seventeen, Eung was in a car accident; as a result, she failed to graduate. For a few years, she drifted between her home and friends' houses, working at various jobs. Through Portland Adult Education, she eventually she got her GED and took a few courses at the University of Southern Maine. Then she went back and got her high-school diploma. She took two years off and then applied to USM officially. When her acceptance arrived, it was the happiest day of her life.

Starting college in 2003, Eung recaptured her drive, throwing herself into leadership roles as a member of the student government association and student senate. Outside of USM, she has advocated for homeless teens, with whose plight she identified as a member of the Cambodian diaspora and because her family had been homeless so often. She has worked with homeless youth at Portland's Preble Street Teen Center and Street Academy, which once helped her on the path to USM. In public forums on campus, in the community, and at the Statehouse, she speaks on issues of homelessness, diversity, and Asian Americans.

"I feel like I'm forty years old sometimes," Eung says. Unlike many typical college students, she had little interest in partying or going on spring break. She was more interested in stability and a better life for herself and her mother, who still toils as a migrant worker, catching temporary jobs in a sea-urchin or seafood factory, or attaching stickers to CDs, or traveling to Lowell for work. In 2008, Eung graduated from USM with a political-science degree. She plans to make her childhood dream come true by studying law and public policy, a joint degree program, so that she can work as a civil-rights or immigration lawyer some day. At law school, she hopes to found a group like her proudest legacy at USM, the Asian American Association & Symposium. Ironically, she was the group's only Asian, other than some Japanese exchange students; most members were white. "Other Asians just want to go to school," she says. In fact, Eung feels cut off from other Cambodians, who usually don't recognize her as one of them from her physical appearance. She believes she may have separated herself from them by having mostly white friends and dating men who are outside the Cambodian community. Her inability to speak Khmer may add to a perception that she is "not Khmer enough," she says.

"I lost a lot of sense of my culture, which I'm trying to get back now. It alienated me from my own kind," says Eung. Another way in which she feels she differs from many other Cambodians is her willingness to tell her immigration story. For many years, she silently carried the emotional pain of her broken, impoverished home life.

"In my family, we don't talk much about our past. It hurts. Part of my American life is to talk about it and honor it," says Eung. She feels a new urgency to find out who she is. After years of working to fit into white mainstream America, that means deepening her identity as an Asian American, in spite of living in the very white state of Maine: "Different Asians are coming here now. I feel like it's history in the making, and I'm part of it."

ABDULLAH PIOUS ALI

"Every change starts with young people," says Pious Ali, who has worked for the past five years as a self-described "foot soldier" on behalf of immigrant youth in Portland. He runs a peer-leader program for the People's Regional Opportunity Program at Riverton Park, a public-housing neighborhood whose residents are largely African refugees. Recently, he founded the Maine Interfaith Youth Alliance, building on his earlier success bringing together Muslim and Jewish young people.

His whirlwind of activities with teens doesn't pay much—he supplements his income with a night job—but he has dived into them with the same high energy he once expended in a very different arena. In his native Ghana, Ali was widely known for his work as a photo-journalist. Whether shooting for the news media, the fashion industry, studio productions, or high-profile events, he was the go-to photographer. He once photographed Queen Elizabeth.

"I never thought I would work for a nonprofit, because I was an entrepreneur. When I started to work with young people, my passion for what I do changed. I'm going to do this, God willing, throughout my life," he says. How Ali came to choose such a different path is a story of drive, adaptation, and commitment.

As a Muslim, Ali belonged to a minority in Ghana, which despite a long tradition of Islam, now has a majority Christian population. His Hausa tribe, who originate from Nigeria, are also a minority in Ghana, a stable West African democracy. As a child, he lived among people of different faiths, including indigenous beliefs; therefore, religious tolerance comes naturally to him, he says. So does being surrounded by kids. Born in Accra, the capital, in 1969, Ali was raised in a small town called Nsawam, a half-hour's drive away. His parents divorced when he was a baby because his paternal grandmother didn't get along with his mother, who later remarried and moved to northern Nigeria.

Ali's maternal grandmother raised him in a household that included not only his large extended family, but also thirty-five to forty kids who boarded at the madrassa (Islamic religious school) his grandfather operated there. Along with the other children, Ali wrote Arabic lessons on a small board in ink made from rice or corn, and memorized passages from the Koran, which he read in its entirety by the age of twelve. From the age of nine, he also attended a Presbyterian/Methodist public school, where instruction was in English, Ghana's lingua franca.

"I was happy. It was a good life. I had all the support a young person needs to grow up healthy," says Ali. His grandmother presided with a firm hand as a kind of community grandmother. "If I had a fight and I was wrong, she would bring me to the other kid's house and beat me," or beat the other child in front of his own family if he was in the wrong, Ali says. "We lived a community life," where adults watched over all the children, not just their own. Meanwhile, Ali maintained a relationship with his father, whom he saw during visits to Accra, until his father's death when Ali was twelve.

Ali's secure, small-town life changed abruptly when his grandmother moved to Accra, where he attended West Africa Secondary School, a tough all-boys' school in the heart of the city of 2.2 million people. What urban life lacked in sense of community, however, it made up for in stimulation, as Ali's world expanded to include different kinds of people and an exciting new interest—photography. Attracted to art but lacking drawing talent, he found his visual arts groove after someone gave him a small camera. Soon he started a photo club, photographed for a youth magazine, and took on paying assignments, along with participating in a theater group—all of which exposed him to a variety of more affluent young people, some of whom wound up in positions of influence beneficial to his budding career. "I became a celebrity photographer. I could walk into any event in Ghana without an invitation," says Ali.

Around this time, he began using the name "Pious" as a nom de plume, out of respect for his Muslim relatives, who might not have approved of his photography on religious grounds. The name came about in high school, when an African history teacher asked him what his first name, Abdullah, meant. When Ali replied, "servant of God," the teacher asked him to research it, and Ali found a further definition, "a pious fellow." The moniker stuck with his classmates and in his new profession.

A university education would have followed secondary school if Ali could have afforded it. However, once his middle-class father died, that possibility vanished. So, while he thrived on his work and travels around Ghana, he wasn't earning much money. At that point, a dream of going to America took hold.

"I wanted a better life economically," says Ali, who had grown adventurous and confident of making his way in the world. "I wanted to go to America; it was a prize. America is like a well-packaged product. It looks very glamorous. If I come here, it means I made it—I'm a man." So, ten years ago, he took off for New York. Once there, reality set in, as he struggled to build a photography career with only a certificate of merit from a Ghanaian photojournalism course. To make ends meet, he also worked in a clothing store and McDonald's, and sold women's hair products, while living in the Bronx.

"It was a little bit dicey," says Ali, who loved New York but began to feel he was losing his soul in a fast-paced place where no one knew anyone else. "There was no time to reflect, no feeling of community." Then, a few years later, he visited Maine, where he met and married his future wife, who is from the state. He found in Maine echoes of the small-town life that nurtured him as a child.

"After I came here, I liked it because of its sense of community. The arts scene also attracted me." But Ali didn't pursue his photography. Instead, he found himself gravitating toward helping young immigrants who faced challenges in their new environment. He had noticed in New York how adults were afraid of young people, and he began to see a positive role for himself with teenagers. As he would have done as an adult in his childhood town of Nsawam, he just started talking to young immigrants, especially African boys. "I talk to everybody—it's my survivor tool. I grew up in a small town where anyone can tell youth what to do. I like to get involved," says Ali.

And so he dived in, applying for a job at People's Regional Opportunity Program, a social-service agency. He works as a peer leader in a Youth Resiliency Program serving some 300 young people a year in four public-housing neighborhoods. Its aim is to create leadership opportunities for middle-school and high-school kids through social activism, arts projects, and volunteering. Students have researched causes of homelessness, written a play, produced a documentary, and volunteered for public events. Some of the boys collaborate with the Boys to Men organization; others do a TV production every year. Ali helps them get jobs, and, if they have a problem at school, he goes to school to advocate for them.

"I see the kids I work with here as my kids," says Ali, who is a father. He and his wife, who works as an office manager, have a son and a daughter. They share a car between them, shuttling among three jobs, since Ali also works four nights a week at a Volunteers of America transitional home for former prisoners on Portland's Brackett Street. If Ali seems to have a hyper work ethic, it may have something to do with his Ghanaian culture, in which a man's honor and reputation are wrapped up in the quality of and attention to his work, regardless of what he does for a living.

An earlier night job at the Preble Street Lighthouse Shelter taught Ali about homeless teens, and since then he has developed a conviction that youth need to be listened to. "I didn't grow up being listened to. In Ghana, kids are seen, not heard. Kids can be timid and respectful in the extreme," says Ali, who described Ghanaian child-rearing practices in an article called "A Man from My Culture" in a Boys to Men newsletter of January 2007:

I am not a friend to my children. I am not too kind or too generous to my children. I am a fair man and I am responsible for disciplining my children because it is my responsibility to prepare them for the world that is beyond my home. . . . It is my wife's responsibility to physically nurture the children. I do not apologize to my children even if I understand that I am wrong. I do not explain myself to my children and I never tolerate a child arguing with me or talking back to me. I can also act as a father to all the children in my neighborhood, whether we are related or not, and I am expected to treat them like my own. . . . I am also a lifelong ambassador of my family, community, and culture.

Ali has come to see that each culture has its positives and negatives. For example, "Here, nobody listens to young people, even though they say a lot," he says. Yet listening is essential to establishing rapport with teens—a conclusion he came to early in his peer-leader job, when the kids tested him until he listened to them and learned more about them. After more than five years of working with young people, Ali has come to another conclusion:

"I believe that young people who have faith—it doesn't matter what kind, and it doesn't have to be organized religion—will do better." To that end, he started an organization called Maine Interfaith Youth Alliance, which welcomes all faiths. He has facilitated events drawing Muslim, Jewish, and Christian youth together to get to know each other and do community work jointly. With seed money from the nonprofit Bread for the Journey and a lot of community support, the alliance is underway.

Although Ali is a devout Muslim who prays five times a day and shuns alcohol, he believes in opening a dialog about common values to everybody, including those not of the Abrahamic faith, such as Buddhists, and even to atheists. "I believe God created people in different genders and races so we would understand each other and know each other better," says Ali, paraphrasing a favorite quote of his from the Koran.

For a former celebrity photographer once welcomed in the highest circles of Ghanaian society, this life of service to disadvantaged youth in his adopted homeland does not really seem so contradictory, considering he grew up in a multifaith environment as one of dozens of children in his own home. Add to those elements the fact that Ali has a talent for adaptation ("a part of me assimilates easily to wherever I find myself," he says), and you find an immigrant who began making a difference in Maine almost as soon as he got here.

"This has become home. So I might as well make this a good place for kids, including my own," he says. Asked what he has given up by leaving Ghana, he answers, "I left a hard-earned, privileged life. But by coming to this country, I've learned a lot that I wouldn't have learned in any classroom."

Note: The peer-leader program for which Ali worked at the time of his interview for this book ended in June 2008 for lack of funding. He has since worked with Seeds of Peace, an international organization bringing together youth from regions of conflict around the world for training in conflict resolution and intensive dialog about race, religion, culture, and economic disparity. A local offshoot, Maine Seeds, was created to respond to rising community tensions following influxes of immigrants to Portland and Lewiston in recent years.

"I believe if the Seeds of Peace program will be introduced in conflict zones all over the world, it will get rid of half of the world's conflicts," says Ali.

Back in Moscow, Jews used to enjoy a little inside joke.

"Who are you?" one would ask.

"I'm a 'fifth,'" another would answer, to laughter.

They were referring to the fifth item on the identification card Soviet citizens carried, the item that listed their nationality as "Jewish." Black humor took the edge off the painful reality that one word could threaten their chances for a better life at every turn, making it hard to get accepted to a certain university, or advance in a job, or worship without fear at a synagogue. Many Jews tried to hide the fact that they were Jewish, consigning their jokes and worried conversation to the kitchens of their homes. Some even changed their papers, a tactic that didn't work because the authorities always knew who was Jewish.

Once they could leave the USSR, starting in the early 1970s, hundreds of thousands of Jews did so, mostly for Israel and the U.S. Lana and Joseph Shkolnik were among them, arriving in this country in 1990. After a year in Louisville, Kentucky, they moved to Portland, where their parents joined them a few years later. Today, Lana relishes no longer needing to hide her identity.

"I can say it out loud, 'I'm a Jew,'" she says.

Even though they had led the kind of largely secular life typical of all citizens in Soviet days, the Shkolniks had suffered religious persecution, which qualified them for refugee status. One word had marked them for discrimination, subtle though it usually was.

"My husband couldn't get into a Ph.D. program even though he passed all the tests, and he was pretty much told, 'This year we're not accepting any Jews,'" says Lana, explaining that various university faculties had quotas on Jews. For example, only three or four might be accepted into a whole faculty of medicine, as her uncle found out when his application to medical school was denied. Joseph certainly had the qualifications, with a record of top marks, a master's degree in computer programming, and a history of working in his field.

"He loves to study, but he didn't get that chance" for a doctorate, says Lana, who describes the corrosive effect such rejections had on Jewish people: "That causes problems inside you; you feel like you're not worthwhile." Job discrimination had the same depressing effect, she says.

"Your I.D. says 'Jewish.' You apply for a job and they say, 'Sorry, it's filled.'"

For instance, when Joseph's mother graduated from college as a production analyst in 1954 in

Odessa, she couldn't find a job, and that could still happen in the 1970s and 1980s, she says. Typically, though, it wasn't difficult for qualified Jews to get hired in most professions; career advancement was the more common problem. Lana cites her father, Arkady ("Archie") Antonovskiy, a gifted engineer who worked on airplane engines and was a creative inventor, but got stuck at a certain career level because he is Jewish.

"He never gets anywhere, so he stays put," she says. When asked if he and other Jews pressed for advancement, she answers, "You don't want to put yourself in a position where they say no." Thus anti-Semitism played itself out in understated, insidious ways. "[They treat you] like a dog on a chain. They let you go, then pull you back."

Ordinary acts like going shopping in a department store could result in anti-Semitic encounters, too. "You're standing in line and someone will approach you and say, 'You're Jewish. Go back to Israel,'" she recalls.

On Jewish high holy days when her family went to their synagogue, it was obvious that security officers were watching, she says. "They were there. You could see them in the corridor. Those eyes go through you. It still gives me the creeps. We didn't go to synagogue as often as we would like to."

Lana grew up in Moscow, where her family would gather at holidays with relatives, the only people with whom they discussed Jewish life. Outside of gefilte fish and matzo, Jewish food and customs were not a focus of family life. Lana graduated from university with a degree in statistics and had no problem getting hired by a small company for a job analyzing statistics for local government. But she did not try to move up in the company because, as she says, "You stay quiet."

Her husband, Joseph, was born in Odessa, a Ukrainian city on the Black Sea that was home to a vibrant Jewish community for generations until World War II. His grandparents were killed when German soldiers wiped out their Jewish village. Joseph came to Moscow for university studies. Once he and Lana married and their son, Kirill, was born, Lana quit her job to stay home. As they pondered their son's future, they decided to leave the USSR. "Our son would have to go into the army. No Jewish mom wants that," says Lana. Also, "in America, he could go to any university he wanted."

After waiting a year for their application to be processed, they were finally approved for emigration. It was 1989, a time when the Soviet Union of reformist Mikhail Gorbachev was about to crumble; the USSR dissolved two years later. Many Soviet Jews had been asking to leave since the 1960s, but couldn't until the "refusenik" era of the 1970s, when Jews publicly protested Soviet refusals of permission to emigrate. In the late 1980s and early 1990s, more than half the Jewish population is estimated to have left for Israel, the U.S., and Germany.

The Shkolniks wanted to go to America, but in order to get permission to leave, they had to say they wanted to immigrate to Israel, since Jews were not allowed to go directly to the U.S. Once approved, they flew to Vienna with Kirill, who was two and a half, taking only their clothing with them. Lana had shipped a small collection of family china ahead.

"It exists!" was Lana's excited reaction upon seeing Vienna. Like other Jews, she had never been able to travel outside her country, although she was well informed about other places from reading, watching TV, and listening to the BBC. Aided by a Jewish group, they stayed in a Viennese suburb for a month until hearing the good news that they were going to the U.S. But first they had to travel to Italy, where U.S. embassy officials would process their applications. On the train to Italy, an eerie episode reminiscent of World War II shook them up when a security officer ordered them to leave the train immediately because many years earlier a similar train carrying Jews had come under attack. They threw their suitcases out the window and left, never finding out the cause of the disruption.

Eventually the Shkolniks reached the small town near Rome that they were assigned to, and stayed for five months while U.S. embassy officials reviewed their application and interviewed them to determine their refugee status.

"It was scary, because we knew some people who were rejected," Lana remembers. But they were approved and told they would be sent to Louisville, Kentucky. They boarded a Pan American flight filled with other Jewish immigrants, and arrived in Louisville to a warm welcome by members of the Jewish community. Lana liked America right away.

"Everything was, 'Wow!' In Russia, there were lines for food, never enough, and not enough variety," Lana says. They were not disappointed that they had to work hard to partake of the plenty. "It didn't occur to us to be disappointed. When we left, we were prepared for the worst. We didn't come here for the money," she says.

After a few months of English-language, cultural-orientation, and job-training classes, Joseph found a computer-programming job at the University of Louisville, and Lana got hired to work in the preschool where their son was enrolled.

A year later, Joseph decided he could find a better job and sent resumes around the country. Soon a headhunter recruited him for a programming job with Hannaford Bros. supermarket company, and the family was off to Portland. It wouldn't have mattered to them where they moved, Lana says, and in fact, the former Muscovite wasn't impressed with Portland when she arrived. "It's so small," she thought.

At first, Lana had a hard time finding a job, so she became a nanny for a few mothers from the Jewish preschool Kirill attended. Later, she worked in a podiatrist's office, and finally settled into the job she has held for fourteen years, accounting clerk at Applicators Sales & Service, a building-products wholesaler in Portland. Meanwhile, Joseph has moved on from Hannaford to consulting for a software company.

Both their careers demonstrate the kind of upward momentum Lana says was hard to attain in the Soviet Union. Their personal life is much improved, too. They attend their local synagogue freely. And their dream of having their son attend any college of his choice came true when Kirill enrolled at Stony Brook University in Long Island, New York, where he studies nanoscale engineering. Unfortunately, Kirill isn't likely to settle here after college. "He doesn't see opportunity here in Maine" for work in his innovative field, says Lana.

The Shkolniks' household is full of life, with regular visits from their parents and the company of several squawking parrots. Lana's stepmother, Galina Antonovskiy, appreciates her quiet life in Maine. "It's good for kids and for old people," she says. After all, she lived through a time when Jews not only endured job discrimination, but also had to run for their lives.

Galina was born in Simferopol, the capital of Crimea, now an autonomous republic of Ukraine, on the northern coast of the Black Sea. She remembers the German occupation of the region during World War II because she and her mother, younger brother, and grandparents had to flee to Siberia when she was four years old to avoid becoming targets for the Germans. Her father died fighting for the Soviet army, leaving behind his young family along with letters from the Front to his wife that Galina treasures. An aunt of Lana's who fought as a partisan was also killed in Crimea, scene of bloody battles and ethnic cleansing during the war.

In Siberia, Galina's family hid with several other families in the basement of a non-Jewish family. Three years later, they were able to return to Crimea and start life over. Galina's mother finished university and became a successful lawyer. In 1949, the family moved to Moscow, where her mother married a lawyer. They were two Jewish lawyers, at a time when it was practically impossible for a Jew to become a lawyer, she says.

Galina grew up to become a chemical engineer, graduating from Moscow University in 1959 and enjoying a forty-year career as head of a laboratory. Although her mother had had to join the Communist Party to continue in her work, Galina never did; nor did Lana. While Galina had a rewarding career, she believes she could have moved into a higher management job if she had not been Jewish. She kept quiet about her religion, because anti-Semitism reared its head unexpectedly and often.

"Many people called us Jews, or put a Star of David on the wall and wrote 'Jews, go away,'" she recalls, adding that Jews weren't the only Soviet citizens who couldn't enjoy a good life under the Soviets.

"Everybody without exception had the same life, Jew or non-Jew—without clothes enough, without food enough, with long lines for shopping," says Galina, who doesn't regard her life in those days as unhappy, since "we didn't know a different life." Today, when Lana and Galina visit Russia, they are impressed with how well people can live if they have money, but saddened to see a huge contrast between rich and poor.

Do the women miss Russia? Lana does miss Moscow's lively cultural scene and bustling streets. Maine may be a little too quiet for her taste, but "it's the best place to raise kids," she says.

"The Russian culture is very rich," says Galina, who particularly misses bookshops; in the Soviet Union, everybody read constantly, even on the subway. However, they have made Maine their home—all the family members are U.S. citizens—and they are happy here, in a place where being Jewish isn't an issue, as it was in the USSR. "Here, you know who you are," Lana says.

TOMAS FORTSON

At the age of seventeen, Tomas Fortson was one of the better young squash players in North America. From then on, national boundaries meant little in an exciting athletic career that bounced back and forth between his native Mexico and New York, Venezuela, London, and Boston, as he played the professional circuit internationally and ran club squash programs. By the time he became men's and women's squash coach at Bowdoin College, he and his wife were ready to settle in a good place to raise their children, and they found it in Brunswick.

The college town on the coast some twenty-five miles northeast of Portland might seem an unlikely setting for someone from Mexico City, the largest city in the Western Hemisphere. How Fortson got to Maine says a lot about the big reputation he acquired over the years in what he calls "the small world" of the game of squash. It also illustrates how a Mexican with an exceptional talent can make a unique contribution on this side of the border. As just one mark of that contribution, he was named New England Small College Athletic Conference Coach of the Year in 2008.

At the time of the Bowdoin offer, Fortson was living with his wife and daughter in Puerto Vallarta, where he was teaching and promoting golf, which he had just picked up. The surprise offer came in October 2000, the day after the birth of his son, bearing out a Mexican saying: "Kids come with a cake" (roughly translated as "A baby brings good luck").

"We didn't think about it for more than ten minutes. We thought it was the best opportunity for our kids," says Fortson, who moved to Brunswick with his family two months later. He didn't have to give up golf for long, since he soon added coaching the men's golf team to his duties.

Fortson's first love, squash, developed early in Mexico City, where he was born in 1962. With the city's population exploding, his family moved to the outskirts when he was ten years old.

"It was really healthy there. There was a new neighborhood development and opportunity for a young family. I was very fortunate; I had a great childhood," says Fortson. His father, an Avon executive, and his homemaker mother provided a stable, middle-class home with two cars and annual family vacations. Fortson was always at the top of his class at school, for which he credits his mother's support. After school, he played out on the streets every day for hours, at a different sport—soccer, baseball, or tennis—each season. Life was good.

"Two years after we moved into the neighborhood, my parents discovered this squash club. We as a family spent a lot of time there. Both my parents played squash," and enjoyed the lively social scene that went with it. "My dad is a big athlete. He played American football in college in Mexico. Whether that came from my grandfather, I don't know," says Fortson, whose grandfather was a "nine-tenths black" American who had gone to Cuba, married a white Cuban woman, and moved to Mexico.

"Dad was one of the top two players in the club. Everybody loved my dad. He left his mark"—especially on his son, who learned from him how to compete. Through his club experiences, Fortson learned about the class context for squash, too.

"Some of the best players coming out of Mexico then were rich people," Fortson says, but his club was a newer type that opened up the game to more people. Unfortunately, as the middle-class clubs spread, wealthier clubs closed. "Those rich kids quit, now that it was mixed. But the middle-class clubs stayed open, and a number of kids developed into top-level players. What's happened now is that there are a ton of pay-to-play clubs in Mexico. Mexican kids are coming to play the U.S. national championships, and they always go back with trophies. The great majority are middle class at best," he says, by contrast with the U.S., where squash remains primarily an elite private sport.

A year later, his father got transferred to White Plains, New York, for his job, and his family moved with him. Fortson, the eldest of five children, had little trouble sliding into life in a large suburban high school, where he immediately made friends among the Peruvian, Chilean, and Puerto Rican students.

"I had taken English in Mexico, but it didn't apply. Sitting in front of TV was by far the best" help in learning English, he says. The family often watched The Brady Bunch and joked that they were like a "Mexican Brady Bunch."

Fortson and his father found a squash club nearby in Mamaroneck, where they quickly became the best players and had some "pretty good battles" against each other as the son gained on the father. "The day I finally beat him, he never beat me again, but it took longer than expected," he says. Fortson was lucky to be living in a state that hosted all the big squash events at a time when he was ready for serious competition. One day, he was thrilled when Sharif Khan, the legendary Pakistani who dominated the North American game of hardball squash in the 1970s, invited Fortson to warm up with him.

After Fortson became the best junior player in New York and won the Insilco B National Championship, Yale and Princeton tried to recruit him for their teams—a development for which he was unprepared. "No one talked to me about college. I had no clue about the process, no SAT preparation. I ended up on the wait list at Yale just because this coach approached me," he says. When he didn't get accepted, he found a job at a big New York City club teaching squash and running the desk.

A year later, a Fordham University coach offered him a scholarship, and he started attending the Bronx campus. However, he was more advanced than his squash teammates, and without the daily challenge, his skills were going downhill. By his third year, he dropped out.

Meanwhile, after another job transfer, his family was living well in a penthouse in Caracas, Venezuela, where Fortson joined them for a time to focus on his squash training. Fortson found the easygoing Venezuelan lifestyle "heaven on earth," if lazy, in contrast to the stronger Mexican work ethic. When the family was transferred back to Mexico, Fortson struck out on his own, for London.

"I had a one-way ticket, $100 in my pocket, found a youth hostel, and started making calls to the clubs," he recalls. Within a week, he landed a job as teaching pro at the Wembley Squash Centre, London's biggest club and training home of greats like Jahangir Khan, the era's dominant world champion. The club manager never brought up the subject of Fortson's working papers until about eight months after he was hired. Learning that he would have to apply from outside England, Fortson chose to quit the job and return to Mexico.

For the next few months, he trained ten hours a day, starting at 6:00 a.m. with a run, on-court drills followed by matches at a club, then workouts at home. He read about other sports such as baseball and tennis to find applications to squash. It was an all-out push toward his goal of returning to the U.S. to hit the professional circuit. "Most Mexicans have very good endurance. It's one of the reasons Mexicans have always been very good at squash," he says.

Only one event broke through his laser-like focus on training—meeting his future wife, Marilu, whom he had spotted at his squash club. One day when his brother had a birthday coming up and they decided to find some dates to go dancing with, Marilu came to mind. "Right then and there" they fell in love, he says. The next couple of years were not easy for them, while she finished college in Mexico and he taught squash at a New York club and played the pro tour.

"I was trying to be the best squash player in the world," says Fortson, who broke into the top twenty. "The process of trying to get yourself into the rankings is one of the most stressful things I've ever done. Every qualifying match is life and death. Once you're in, the matches are easier to handle."

Two years into this high-pressure life, he and Marilu married and moved in 1989 to the Boston neighborhood of Allston, where he worked as the head professional in one of the largest squash clubs in the country. Owned by a squash player, the "squash cathedral" hosted several major tournaments per year and regularly hosted national championships. Marilu became a good player herself and helped out in the pro shop while Fortson taught, toured, and ran the club's program.

After he spent eight years in this job, the club fell victim to two developments. The first was conversion from hardball, the game played in the U.S., Canada, and Mexico, to softball, the version played everywhere else and the one that will be played if squash becomes an Olympic sport. North American clubs had to make their courts two feet wider for softball, which is a tougher game physically and harder on older players. At the time, the two games' professional associations were merging into the Professional Squash Association, and from Fortson's high-visibility position in Boston, he advocated for playing both. Eventually, though, his club's hardball events dwindled, and they lost older players.

The second development was the club's financial problems, which resulted in the elimination of Fortson's job and sale of the club to the New York Sports Club chain.

"I was never too concerned. We would land on our feet regardless," he thought. Looking back on it, though, Fortson believes they made a mistake during their Boston years by not obtaining an employer-sponsored green card, which allows a person to live and work permanently in the U.S. "We kept switching visas back and forth and talked to a ton of attorneys, and in the end the green cards never materialized," says Fortson, whose exceptional athletic ability had always qualified him for temporary work visas. "It was a mistake that we paid for later on."

The Fortsons were thrilled with his next job offer: squash and racquetball pro in a large club in Las Vegas, where they would live in one of the city's new family-friendly developments. "It was paradise out there. It was very exciting for us to go there—only to find out after we bought a home that the club was owned by the developers," who sold it to a fitness club franchise which dropped Fortson's position. The next blow came when Fortson's application for a green card was rejected because he lost the job on which it was based. "We had the option of staying there illegally, but we didn't want to do that. We started to think about going back to Mexico."

But Fortson's luck in attracting job offers held, and they wound up at Groton School, a Massachusetts prep school, where he taught squash for a year. At a match one day, he heard that Bowdoin College was looking for a squash coach. Fortson came to the campus to interview, but someone else was chosen. With that, the family moved back to Mexico. They spent the next two and a half years happily living in Puerto Vallarta, where their son was born in 2000 and they spent time with family, including his two sisters. (His two brothers live in the U.S., both working as computer engineers.) Fortson had gotten into the golf scene and was about to sign on to a tempting new job, when a call came from Bowdoin: the job had reopened, and would he like it?

"The attraction was that this was a perfect setting. We were fully in the mode of finding the best place for our family. We knew we didn't want Mexico City. I had seen Maine. I thought, 'We can't find a better place to bring our kids up in a healthy, safe environment,'" says Fortson. Except for the lack of spring, he and his family like Maine, and he finds his campus job highly rewarding.

"The quality of the students that come to Bowdoin is the key element. They hunger for achievement, knowledge, and doing things well," says Fortson, whose men's and women's teams perform well competitively. Most of the student players come from affluent backgrounds, reflecting the traditional image of American squash as an East Coast, private-school phenomenon. He would like to see more financial aid offered to international student squash players to help broaden the game demographically. He welcomes the fact that the game is attracting more underprivileged youth in cities in recent years and does his part to expand its popularity, running summer squash camps and hosting tournaments.

While Fortson seems to have sailed through his transnational career, the issue of working papers has dogged him. Over the years, he and his wife have applied for "visa after visa after visa," in at least one case receiving an incorrect visa from a lawyer and having to travel to Mexico to sort out the mess. The green card he now holds could be the first step toward becoming a U.S. citizen. But that decision will not be taken lightly.

"My concern would be our status as a country, and would we go to war. I just don't believe in war. We have a tendency here to push as hard as we can in the world, and the U.S. gets involved in wars all the time. Part of the culture here is to put your life on the line," in contrast to Mexico's culture, he believes. But Mexico has its downside, too, he says, citing the corruption and inefficiency to which he was exposed in his job as tennis-club manager. With mixed ancestry because of his American grandfather, and more than four decades lived alternately on both sides of the border, Fortson is torn between the two countries.

"Half my blood is American," he says. "We have close ties to our families in Mexico. Mexico is great. We always had that temptation to go back, and still have it." Yet in the end, since Mexico changed its law to allow dual citizenship, he and his wife will probably pursue U.S. citizenship, he says, conferring on Maine the benefit of his leadership in the game of squash for years to come.

ISMAIL AHMED

On the banks of the Androscoggin River in Lewiston, overlooking the cascading Great Falls, sits a cluster of abandoned brick mills and the old Central Maine Power office building—all slated for redevelopment into a multi-use complex showcasing the city's western gateway. The project represents an optimistic statement in a city known to the rest of the U.S. in news coverage primarily as a depressed town whose welcome to Somali immigrants was, at best, mixed. Now one of those Somalis runs his own business in the CMP building, himself a symbol of the potential for regeneration the immigrants offer this city that was built by earlier Franco-American immigrants.

Ismail Ahmed opened his S.T.T.A.R. (Support, Training, Technical Assistance and Resources) agency in 2007 to help refugees become self-sufficient. A consultant with a master's degree in leadership and organizational studies from the University of Southern Maine's Lewiston-Auburn College, he provides what he remembers needing most when he arrived in the U.S.—English and workplace-skills training. His business card depicts a figure climbing a tall ladder into a sunny blue sky, illustrating Ahmed's belief that refugees can be highly productive, if only the skills they bring with them can be translated into American ones. He understands their needs because he has climbed that ladder himself, rung by rung, propelled by a love of learning and an independent, contrarian spirit.

Ahmed has made a name for himself as an outspoken advocate for Lewiston's immigrant community. Less than a year after arriving there, he joined others in calling for then-mayor Laurier Raymond's resignation following Raymond's now infamous letter asking Somalis to stop moving to the city and overwhelming its services. Ahmed's conflict-resolution efforts have earned him leadership awards, and his drive has brought him to the point of starting his for-profit business, without the help of loans, just six years after moving to Maine.

What accounts for his rapid success? According to Ahmed, the answer to that question goes back to his childhood.

"I was always free-thinking. My mother was progressive, and my father was open-minded," he says. Ahmed was born in Mogadishu in 1972 to parents who placed a high value on education. Although his mother was illiterate, she sat with her children while they did their homework. Ahmed's father, a junior clerk in a local council, exhibited a yen for learning and knew English and Arabic, a mark of an educated Somali.

But the family had misfortune. "At an early age, I knew people were talking about my family. They felt nothing would come of us because we were very poor," Ahmed says. The pain of their attitude lingered, providing one explanation for his motivation and achievements. "I think it's my fear of failure. My worry is, what happens if I prove them right?" As a university student in Somalia, he was headed for the teaching profession. The Somali civil war put a violent end to that plan in 1991, when troops closed in on the Mogadishu area. Ahmed's family moved to an uncle's house for a time, until the fighting around them escalated.

"I said, 'Mom, we have to get out of here!'" he recalls. Ahmed, his mother, and his four siblings had to leave abruptly one day, at a time when his father had not been able to return home. For a month they roamed "helter-skelter, all over the place," then fled by boat in February 1992 for a Kenyan refugee camp in Mombasa, southwest of Mogadishu on the Indian Ocean.

Ahmed, in his early twenties, was about to acquire an education far different from his university studies. Coming from a 99 percent Somali Muslim society, he was impressed with Mombasa's multilingual, multifaith population of Africans, Arabs and Indians, and curious about how Kenya functioned as a republic. Eager to learn more, he left for Nairobi, the capital, a year and a half later. "I had to get away," says Ahmed.

That wasn't easy, since he lacked proper documents and got stopped repeatedly by the police. ("You just bribe your way," he says.) In Nairobi, his biggest problem was lack of English and Swahili, which he tried picking up from the market, TV, and newspapers, especially the Sunday papers' children's section and puzzles. He also went to a Catholic Church school and appealed to the nuns, who taught him in the convent.

"They respected me and embraced me. It was my first time to interact with other religions," says Ahmed. He intensified his English study by reading on his own and lightened his lessons by turning often to his favorite section of the *Reader's Digest*, "Laughter Is the Best Medicine."

A chance meeting with a wealthy Kenyan continued his lucky streak when the man offered him a job as his driver, and Ahmed wound up being virtually adopted by the man's family. Living in comfortable servants' quarters in their household in an elite suburb of Nairobi, he observed the successful life of a well-educated CFO of a multinational company.

"It exposed me again to my burning desire for education," Ahmed says. The job allowed him to bring his mother, siblings, and other relatives to Nairobi's outskirts and support them all. It also offered enough free time to stop by the British Council library and read. Eventually, he could speak English and Swahili well enough to engage his flair for advocacy.

"I got politicized in Kenya. The marketplaces were alive with political discourse," says Ahmed. Then, as now, he didn't hesitate to speak out about refugee rights. He thought there must be a better way to deal with refugees than expel them from Africa.

"Bring refugees in, give them skills, temporary work permits. Put us in areas where we can be productive," was his pitch to the UN High Commissioner for Refugees and international nongovernmental organizations. His mother cautioned him to mind his own business, since

Kenya wasn't his own country. "I'd say, 'I can't do anything about my country. I love *this* country. We know we messed up our country, there's no excuse for it. But we still have rights,'" he says.

Having accumulated seven years of valuable work experience, Ahmed was well prepared when his chance to immigrate to the U.S. came in 1999. Unfortunately, his family was split up because they were not a refugee "family package" with a mother and children under the age of twenty-one. His mother and older sister went to England, his older brother went with an aunt to Europe, and his younger sister remained in Kenya for a time. Ahmed's only option was Atlanta, Georgia, where his younger brother had gone three years earlier. "Life is good here," reported his brother. At first, Ahmed agreed with that assessment.

"It was wonderful. The economy was good, and there were good communities of African Americans," he observed. Soon, however, he discovered other neighborhoods where people lived in violence-plagued projects—not unlike Nairobi's dangerous streets.

Ahmed's first job, fulfilling orders for computer-assembly companies, introduced him to the fast-paced American workplace. Some of his co-workers' attitudes puzzled him—for example, an African American who thought of Africa stereotypically as a jungle full of wild animals, and a white Gulf War veteran who expressed left-wing, antiwar opinions. To find a context for what he was hearing, Ahmed surfed the Internet on his brother's computer. He took adult-education classes on top of his day job, an evening job at Pep Boys, and a weekend job at Wal-Mart.

Next came a job packaging CDs, working alongside other Somalis and a larger group of Latinos, who spoke no English. "The workplace was volatile," he says, due to the poor relationship between the two groups and the high-pressure, assembly-line work atmosphere. "It is good that I worked on that level. I felt I was fulfilling that part of the American dream ritual."

Ahmed's third job, as an exterminator for a pest-control company, held more lessons on American race relations. "I was given some of the poor white clients. Most white employees were given upper-class whites," says Ahmed. He was surprised when poor white people showed him Southern hospitality, giving him a drink and a cookie when he arrived. Yet where he expected a friendly welcome, at the homes of affluent African Americans, he rarely got one. A more disturbing reaction surfaced at the time of the September 11 attacks, when a wary white homeowner asked him if he was a Muslim and told him to spray only the outside of the house.

At the time Ahmed arrived in Georgia, citizens were debating removing the Confederate flag from the state capital, and Ahmed struggled to understand the racially charged issue. "I started thinking, 'What side should I be on?'" he says. The question was part of a larger search for his own identity in his new culture.

"African Americans would say, 'Don't trust those [white people]. Slavery is our heritage.' When I was with white clients, they would say, 'Don't be like the African Americans. Don't be bitter. Just work hard. The flag is our heritage,'" says Ahmed, who couldn't have been working harder at getting ahead.

"I felt I was productive. America was offering me a chance," he says. Still, he longed for more education. Noticing diplomas from northeastern universities on the walls of some of his clients' big houses, he enrolled in courses at the local high school and began thinking about moving north for college. By now, his sister and her two children had joined his brother and him in Atlanta.

"Eventually, my sister and I had to decide where to go," says Ahmed. Both were divorced. His brother knew a Somali who had just moved to Maine as one of several thousand "secondary migrants" who had settled first in large American cities and were now opting for safer, smaller environments with affordable housing, like Lewiston and Portland. Once Ahmed read on the Internet about Lewiston–Auburn College's leadership program, he voted for Lewiston and moved there in December 2001. His brother and sister joined him later.

"By the time I arrived here, I knew what I wanted," says Ahmed. To sharpen his academic skills, he took adult-education and undergraduate courses at Lewiston–Auburn College while working at a call center. The second phase of his new life in America looked promising.

He remembers thinking, as he formed his first, favorable impressions of Lewiston, "This is really rural America. I've seen American life closely now and had my first Thanksgiving with a white family. I see big, extended families. There are closer families here" than in Atlanta. Then came the shock of the mayor's letter, exposing Lewiston's frustration at the influx of Somalis—some 1,000 of whom had settled in the small city in the space of eighteen months. After publicly calling for the mayor's resignation, Ahmed set about trying to calm the waters between refugees and city leaders. With his gregarious nature and quick sense of humor, he easily formed relationships around town. He joined the Lewiston Rotary Club and Toastmasters International, and participated in numerous cross-cultural forums, honing his skills as a cultural bridge.

On campus, he co-founded the International Student Organization of Lewiston-Auburn, created an education series on Africa, assisted in planning a study-abroad program to Botswana and South Africa, and earned several USM diversity and leadership awards. In 2005, he became the first graduate of the college's master's program in leadership studies.

Ahmed's next two jobs put that degree to use—first at Lutheran Immigration Services' Refugee Works in Baltimore, and then at Catholic Charities Maine's Refugee and Immigration Services as a cultural-skills trainer.

"It was a tough job; I had to do a lot of PR with landlords, schools, etc. I tried to cool things over," says Ahmed, who was constantly getting phone calls with complaints such as, "The Somalis are running red lights!" Having openly suggested that service providers only addressed refugees' physical, but not emotional, needs, he found that the job gave him a chance to prove himself "as somebody different from how the community portrayed me, as a privileged whistle-blower."

By September 2007, Ahmed was ready to put all he had learned into his own consulting business, working with service providers, employers, and institutions of higher learning. In the spacious second-floor office of the old brick CMP building, he plans to put desks and computers once he secures more collaboration with community agencies. For now, he runs the program himself, with the help of one paid assistant, some student interns, and volunteers.

Ahmed is busier than ever with community activities, serving on the board of Empower Lewiston, Lewiston–Auburn College's citizens' advisory board, and Lewiston–Auburn Neighborhood Network, among others. By now, about 3,500 Somalis have come to the city of 37,000. He believes that relations between the immigrants and the city are okay, but could be better if city leaders and officials altered their approach.

"They think they're doing a great job. 'How dare you question us?'" describes their attitude, he says. Despite their good intentions in trying to serve individual groups' needs, the result is often refugees pitted against each other and nonprofit agencies bickering among themselves, says Ahmed, who takes a more global view that all refugees have similar basic needs and agencies should map integration strategies together as one. He believes that if refugees are invested in, they become an asset to Lewiston, which was losing population before the Somalis arrived, but is now one of the few Maine cities gaining population.

Among the young people bringing diversity to town are Ahmed's niece and nephew. Ahmed devotes a lot of time to assisting his sister, who works as a certified nurse's aide, and her children. "I've tried to bring them up with an open mind," he says, reflecting what his parents taught him. "I'm a bit pro-women, and that puts me into trouble with my culture." His niece plays lacrosse and field hockey at her high school. She and her brother serve on the civil-rights team at school and know how to stand up for their rights. Americanized as they are, Ahmed wonders at what point they will explore their Somali identity and perhaps want to go to Africa.

"The identity issue is very burdening," says Ahmed, who never considered himself black until coming to the U.S. "In Somalia, I was Somali," as well as a clan member and citizen of a nation that had won its independence from colonial powers. "I came to realize that I was seen in America as young, Muslim, black, and Somali . . . in a threatening way or a sympathetic, demeaning way." On the other hand, to some in the Somali community, he is not Somali enough. But controversy has never held Ahmed back. His firm belief that people can be brought together if they "lay everything on the table" and work together for a better community drives him forward. His commitment to helping other immigrants and his love for teaching suffuses his work with refugees learning strange new American ways.

"I'm flexible," says Ahmed, who excuses students who can't do their homework because of responsibilities in their large families. But he makes sure they understand American cultural values so they can climb that ladder to self-sufficiency shown on his business card.

"I tell them, 'Reduce the time spent in the afternoon drinking tea and chit-chatting. Time is money now. This is a competitive world.'"

LAURA VAL

"Why do we need borders?" Laura Val wondered as a young child in Romania. Today, having lived in three different countries and formed an identity as a "global nomad," she is still asking that question. In Maine she believes she has found a place to document the richness of human experience and promote cultural awareness. To that end, she has developed Celebrating Human Creativity, a nonprofit organization based in Portland that will provide a web-based global media resource to schools and youth organizations.

"I see Maine as the state of peace," the last state of the northeastern U.S., virtually reaching out to the rest of the world, she says.

After nine years working for Clark University in Worcester, Massachusetts, when Val's son graduated from high school and left for college, she decided to give herself a gift by moving to Maine to follow her passion for photography. Since she loved hearing people's stories, she soon moved from photography into video documentaries.

To her, "Maine has everything"—beauty, ocean, mountains, culture, and proximity to Boston—and in Portland, she finds a pleasingly small city with a diverse population. While the city has attracted a growing number of people working in the creative arts in recent years, few of them have made quite the journey to get here that Val has, emigrating from Romania to Israel to the U.S. Those very personal journeys inform the work she does today.

Born in Bucharest in 1960, Val spent the first thirteen years of her life in Romania "before the terrible times," as she puts it—the calm before the downward spiral of the despotic Ceausescu regime that precipitated its overthrow in 1989. To her as a child, life in the capital city seemed good, with its social culture centered on family and friends. Her mother, a film editor in Romanian television, and her father, an engineer, divorced when she was just a year old, and he eventually moved to the U.S. with his family. But Val enjoyed a lively family life that included gatherings with her grandparents. On weekends, they went fishing at a nearby lake, or ice-skating, or out to dinner at places where gypsy music was playing and her grandfather taught her to dance the tango and the waltz. She came to love dancing, sang in the school choir, and, like other students in the Communist state, belonged to the Young Pioneers. One of her favorite toys was a toy astronaut, and for a time she wanted to be an astronaut or a dancer when she grew up.

When a teacher asked her on the first day of school if she was Jewish, Val went home and asked, "Mom, am I Jewish?" "Yes," her mother answered. Val had not been raised in

Judaism, and had no Jewish friends. As a child, she wasn't aware of anti-Semitism. Although during the 1960s, the Romanian Jewish community experienced a fairly benign mixture of freedom and government limitations, the pull of aliyah (immigration to Israel) was strong. The Jewish community had shrunk drastically through successive waves of emigration. In fact, Romanian Jews accounted for one of the highest numbers of immigrants to Israel from anywhere in the world. Today, only 15,000 Jews are estimated to live in Romania. Val and her mother joined the emigration in 1973, after waiting three years for permission to leave. Some of their family were already living in Israel.

"I was excited. For me it was an adventure," Val recalls. Her immediate and pressing challenge was to fit into a new culture as a young teenager. Resettlement went smoothly, beginning with a stay in Haifa at an immigrants' center offering excellent language and cultural training and social services. People were welcoming and warm. When the Yom Kippur War broke out a few months after they arrived, sirens would sound sometimes, and Val and her mother and everyone in their building had to run to the safety of the basement of the apartment building in the middle of the night. "Oh, this is what war feels like!" she remembers thinking.

"You feel immediately Israeli" after you arrive, says Val, who was struck by Israelis' openness and informality. After three months, she was placed in a regular school. There, unlike in Romania, she could just speak up and call teachers by their first names. She noticed how young people participated fully in adult social and political discussions. She had to learn Hebrew, whose lack of a formal "you" pronoun made communication sound jarringly direct at first, compared to Romanian, with its formal and informal "you" forms. Israelis seemed to speak more assertively than did the more cautious Romanians she had grown up with.

At thirteen, it wasn't easy to learn a whole new language, culture, and approach to daily living in a more fast-paced, open society than she was used to. She encountered supermarkets for the first time, and was shocked to see Mercedes used for taxis, rather than for government officials as they had been in Romania. Musical and literary tastes differed from the European ones she had been immersed in. She figured out that if she wanted to become part of Israeli culture, she would need to start hanging out with people born in Israel, instead of sticking together with other Romanian young people. Although she missed her good friends back in Romania, she never felt sorry she had moved to Israel. Gradually, she incorporated both Romanian and Israeli cultural nuances into her identity. "My collectivistic part is Romanian. My individualistic part is Israeli," she says.

As a teen, Val had a lot of outlets for her growing creative interests, taking trips, studying ceramics and dance, and joining a poetry club. She was active in an Israel/Arab club where students visited Arab families on the outskirts of Jerusalem and donated clothing to needy families.

After high school, like all young Israelis, Val served in the army. Although she had wanted to do something completely different, like driving a tractor, she wound up working in a library, which suited her just as well. For the first time in her life, she got to know people from many different social and economic backgrounds.

"In Israel, people are coming from different cultures. You are exposed to a wide diversity. When you are outside Israel, everyone asks you, 'Are you Jewish?' In Israel, everyone asks, 'Where are you from?'" she says.

Val married, and four years later had a son, Eviatar. She graduated from Hebrew University in Jerusalem with a degree in art history and Eastern Asian studies, a field to which she was attracted for its exoticism and Taoist influence. The marriage ended in an amicable divorce, so when her ex-husband got a fellowship in Worcester, Massachusetts, she and their son joined him in 1991. It was important to her that in spite of the divorce, her son would have both his parents involved in his life.

And so Val's days in Israel came to an end. Once again, she needed to adjust to a new culture. Although she had learned textbook English, speaking it was difficult. "I couldn't open my mouth for the first three months," she says. "It was that fear of making a mistake." American social communication baffled her at first, with its breezy friendliness. "How are you?" people would ask, without waiting for an answer, or they would meet each other for a lunch break of exactly one hour, but not longer. She noticed that most American youth did not participate actively in the kind of political discourse she was used to in Israel.

Once in the U.S., she found that certain Jewish traditions took on new importance for her, partly for her son's sake. She had been raised in her Bucharest home without Jewish traditions, putting up a Christmas tree at Christmastime as a Romanian cultural expression. In Israel, she found that one did not need to practice religion in order to feel Jewish. The whole country celebrated the Jewish holidays together. You did not have to work hard to feel Jewish; it was taken for granted. In the U.S., for the first time, she started to go to synagogues and actively celebrate the Jewish holidays.

"I was born Jewish, but on a very personal level, I feel that my religion is humanism," she says.

Needing to focus on parenting and earning a living, she worked at a job she found in health care and picked up a master's degree in library science from Simmons College in Boston. A request from Clark University in Worcester for her to consult on a bilingual graduate program for Israeli students led to a job as assistant director of the program, offering her scope for developing her project-management and intercultural communication skills for the next eight years.

Over time, as her son was moving closer to finishing high school, Val explored two paths that would eventually meet in the work she does today. The first was specialized education in interculturalism. The second was training in photography and documentary video, which she studied at Rockport College, an international school for photography, filmmaking, and visual arts in Rockport, Maine. Val fell in love with Rockport and Camden. When Eviatar left Worcester for Northwestern University, she decided to act on one of the lessons Israel had taught her: to be "daring." Letting go of her son as he embarked on his own next stage of life, she quit her job at Clark and moved to Camden. While people found it shocking for her to walk away from a secure, full-time job, she thought of it as a gift to herself.

Although Maine presented another culture shock, with its slower pace of life, she found it welcoming. It met her requirements for a place she wanted to make her home. Developing her own company, Vision in Action, VIA Documentaries, she produced and directed training and documentary videos for nonprofit, corporate, and educational clients. One of those projects was *What Is 6,000,000?*—a documentary about the unconventional teaching methods of a high-school English teacher in rural Maine who uses the Holocaust as a model to teach human responsibility.

Val loves Maine as the background for her creative vision, yet the state's long winters present a challenge. Her solution is trips to warm places in winter—for example, one she took in 2008 to Morocco, which led to a second one months later to give a presentation on communicating effectively across cultures. She had planned for her longtime dream of going to Morocco to come true later. Suddenly, in the new spirit lifting her, she just decided, "Why wait?"

Three years ago, Val moved to Portland to be closer to Boston. She is now focusing her work on her nonprofit, whose purpose is to promote cross-cultural understanding and inspire civic engagement.

"I believe that differences between people should be seen as a source of celebration rather than a threat or a source of conflict," she says. "This is like my second child. It took me years to believe I can do it. I am a woman of forty-eight, and I can do it. I feel the urgency to contribute to the human condition."

TIMWAH LUK

Timwah Luk didn't have to leave his native land to find economic opportunity. There was plenty of that in Hong Kong. But he had a yen to travel as a teenager, and once he came to the U.S., he stayed. Growing up in a bustling, confident city of skyscrapers and sophisticated commerce, Luk was better equipped than many immigrants for life in the West, and once he got his Ph.D. in electrical engineering, he could have found work anywhere in the world.

As it turned out, he chose Maine in 1982, and Fairchild Semiconductor in South Portland has had the benefit of his expertise ever since. Luk's story offers an example of how talent and education can trump national borders in a globalized, high-tech world. It also shows how one immigrant with an open heart can make a difference in his new home.

Today, Hong Kong is a special administrative region of the People's Republic of China. But when Luk was growing up in the 1950s and 1960s, it was a crown colony of the United Kingdom—a onetime British trading post turned financial giant. A bastion of laissez-faire capitalism, Hong Kong has become the freest economy in the world and undergone rapid urbanization.

Since before the British came in the 1840s, Luk's family had lived on Hong Kong Island, the most densely populated of the colony's complex of islands and peninsulas in the South China Sea. His grandfather was a farmer and sometime fisherman. When Luk was a young child, his family lived in the eastern end of the island, in a green area on the edge of the city, in a Boy Scout camp where his father served as the caretaker.

"It was quite fun. We were the only family there," he recalls. Except for the camp's large population of poisonous snakes, it was an idyllic spot removed from city clamor. "Now, it's a subway station—an island surrounded by forty-story buildings," says Luk. When he was fourteen, his family left the camp for an apartment building in the center of the city.

Luk's upper-middle-class parents ran a successful Chinese restaurant where Luk helped out. Religion entered his life early on, when his mother converted to the Roman Catholic faith. He describes his father, who was not religious, as open-minded and more influenced by the West. Their son had the benefit of a high-quality education in Catholic boys' schools whose teachers were priests and nuns from all over the world. In such a cosmopolitan environment, it was hardly surprising that he chose to study abroad when he graduated.

"I always wanted to come to America. I wanted to see the world," he says. After researching colleges in search of a good, affordable school that was competitive in engineering, he chose Iowa State University. Arriving in Ames, Iowa, in March 1974 from the crowded, hot streets of Hong Kong, he took his first look at his new home: miles of plowed, wintry fields still sprinkled with snow. He was to remain there contentedly for the next eight years, until he received his Ph.D. in electrical engineering.

"I liked the people there," says Luk, who found them friendly and helpful. Welcomed at the airport by Chinese Christians, he soon became active in their Bible-study group, which was popular among the campus's several hundred Chinese students. There on campus he met his future wife, who is from a Taiwanese family that immigrated to Singapore; she was studying statistics and computer science. When he graduated, they decided to find work near Boston, where she had relatives—hence his interview at Fairchild Semiconductor.

Luk remembers fondly that he started his new job in South Portland on his first wedding anniversary. Now, more than twenty-five years later, he is a senior director at the company, a global supplier of high-performance semiconductor products. He holds five patents for different methods of designing and fabricating circuits, and he oversees the company's mathematical modeling and computer-aided design (CAD). "We deal with equations that are sixteen pages long," he laughs.

Luk and his wife have built a good life in Maine, centered in family and church. They have raised two children—a son who is doing research in microbiology at Boston College and planning to get his doctorate, and a daughter who is studying at the University of West Virginia to become a pharmacist. They have conveyed strong educational aspirations to their children, as his own parents did to him. When Luk was a child, his mother told him she hoped he would graduate from college, which made a deep impression on him.

"I told my son, 'You can study anything you want, as long as you get a Ph.D.,'" he says, half-jokingly. "Chinese parents have high expectations." That cultural value can be seen in Luk's own Fairchild team of fifty people worldwide, which includes three other Chinese engineers with doctorates, and in his Chinese church, in which at one time all the men had Ph.D.s or M.D.s.

Luk's spacious suburban home in Falmouth pays homage to his culture in its Chinese artwork, and to his family values in its history of housing members of his extended family for a decade when he was busy raising his children and building his career. At one time, his widowed mother and mother-in-law lived there together for a few years—one speaking Cantonese and the other Mandarin, but both forming a deep friendship across the linguistic divide. His older sister and her two sons joined the household for a few years, and his younger sister, who had been diagnosed with cancer, came to live with them, too. When she died, Luk's mother returned to Hong Kong with Luk's older sister, leaving behind gifts born of her love of gardening in a sunroom filled with fruit trees and other large plants, some of which she had started from seeds carried from Hong Kong.

Besides family, the other main focus of Luk's life in Maine has been leadership of a growing community of Chinese immigrants in the Chinese Gospel Church of Portland, where he has done everything from lead Sunday services to host a baptism in the indoor lap pool at his home. When he started the nondenominational church in 1996, it had just three families and held services in borrowed space in a Baptist church in Portland. By the time the members bought their own church a decade later—two buildings on four acres of land in Cumberland—they had become a congregation of some thirty adults and twenty children. Still too small to have its own pastor, the congregation invites visiting ministers from other churches, or Luk takes the lead. Services are in Mandarin, with wireless translation to English available for non-Chinese members, including spouses of mixed marriages. Mandarin is also taught in a language school on Sunday afternoons.

The church grew out of a Bible-study group Luk started on his arrival in Maine. Most of its members were Vietnamese at first, reflecting the Southeast Asian refugee influx to the state in the early 1980s. Since then, Chinese immigrants have come in growing numbers. Some own Chinese restaurants, of which there were only a few in the Portland area when Luk arrived; now there are at least twenty. But if in an earlier time Mainers tended to associate Chinese immigrants exclusively with restaurants, by now they have met many others in the ranks of the medical, engineering, and other professions throughout the state. Luk estimates that a few hundred Chinese professionals live in the Portland area alone.

Besides helping new members with interpreting and other services, the church reaches across the world to help strangers. One example is the case of a baby in northwest China who was born with a heart defect. The baby's mother had traveled across the country with her daughter to Shanghai seeking medical expertise, only to be told she was inoperable. A doctor in Shanghai who had worked in Portland contacted surgeons at Maine Medical Center, who operated on her successfully, free of charge, while church members took care of the mother.

Luk is also proud of the church's involvement with Central Africa Vision, a missionary group he helped organize along with its founder, Rev. Mutima Peter (a Congolese immigrant), and other concerned Maine citizens. Since 1997, the group has raised hundreds of thousands of dollars for victims of war in Rwanda, Burundi, and the Democratic Republic of Congo to promote reconciliation, provide relief, and fund small business loans to widows through community banks. Many of the group's board members have visited the program in central Africa. "They are like my neighbors," Luk says of the war victims.

It is obvious that he feels a compassionate connection with people of other races and faiths—perhaps a legacy of his father's open-mindedness and his mother's spirituality, as well as the experience of growing up in an international crossroads. Luk returns often to the city of his youth, moving easily between Hong Kong and mainland China with a "smart card" system he finds superior to U.S. passport control. These days, China seems so open and business-oriented that it is hard for him to distinguish its lifestyle from that of Hong Kong. In fact, like many elderly Hong Kong citizens, his mother prefers to live in the Cantonese area of China just across the border, because it is greener and prettier.

"Now Communist China is quite tolerant. I go to China a lot. I don't think they are Communist," says Luk, in that "Communist" is just the name of the ruling political party, and no longer the ideology of the people. Hong Kong, too, has changed. When he goes back, he can hardly recognize it. He is struck by how fast buildings go up in a place with much less government regulation than in the U.S. Another change since his childhood is that since the British transferred Hong Kong's sovereignty to China in 1997, it has become more democratic, with more elected representatives in the local government than allowed under the British.

Despite the positive changes in the region, Luk wouldn't consider returning there to live. Having raised his children in Maine and contributed in meaningful ways to his profession and his community, he will stay in his chosen state.

"I like Maine. It's not so crowded. I went back to Hong Kong and said, 'How could I live here? It's so hot, the air conditioning is so cold.' It's slower here, more relaxed, and pretty," he says. He can look outside the large windows of his Falmouth home to a beautifully landscaped garden with a waterfall and pond, or tend the plants in the sunroom so carefully nurtured by his mother, or walk through the woods beyond to the ocean.

"I'm comfortable in China, Hong Kong, and here. But this is home for me," he says. "Even with all the problems we have in America, I think it's a great country."

JELILAT OYETUNJI

Ironically, coming to the small city of Portland helped turn Jelilat Oyetunji into a cosmopolitan person. Arriving at twenty-four with one identity, as a Nigerian college student, she found herself a decade later with a broader one, as a Muslim woman who thinks across national borders and speaks with a strong and effective voice for change. Along the way, she has searched deeply inside herself to find out who she is and what her place in the world should be.

As the crucible for her personal and professional transformation, Maine has given Oyetunji much, she believes. Anyone who knows her would say she has given a lot back, too. The flags from many countries hanging in the University of Southern Maine's cafeteria and the female-only swim times for Muslim women at the former Portland YWCA both came about at Oyetunji's urging. In her 2002 USM commencement speech, she promised, "We will share with the rest of the world the gift that USM has bestowed on us by respecting the diversity that we are going to encounter." She has carried through on that promise through her scholarship and her leadership in interfaith and diversity activities.

One of Oyetunji's most immediate contributions has been her own example, beginning with the day she arrived on campus wearing a *hejab*, or Muslim head covering. The only student to do so at the time, she got curious looks and questions both on and off campus. At first, she couldn't believe people were unfamiliar with the custom.

"All of a sudden, people would walk up and ask me about it. Sometimes people would not just ask politely, but snicker and say, for example, 'Oh, it must be hot under that thing,'" says Oyetunji, who recalls a time when someone in a car snapped a photograph of her standing outside her dormitory on Portland's Congress Street and drove off. "Another time, someone asked me, 'Can I take a picture of you?' I said, 'No! I'm not a tourist attraction.'" Hurtful as such incidents were, they forced her to deal with a challenge she had never had to confront in Nigeria, whose citizens practice Muslim, Christian, and other faiths, and where Muslim women wear a wide range of traditional and Western clothing, with or without *hejab*. Nor had she ever come up against racial barriers.

"I was thrust into this sense of being an 'other.' I never knew what it meant to be a minority before. I was now part of a group because of skin color and oppression. That was hard," she says. Yet if she had stayed home in Nigeria in the comfort of family, friends and everything familiar, she wouldn't have worked as hard as a student, she believes. "I had to prove to myself that I would accomplish what I came here to accomplish."

Oyetunji came to USM for a computer-science degree, which placed her in another minority position, as a female in a male-dominated field. But that role happened to be familiar to her from her years as a math/science student in Nigeria. Furthermore, her parents had encouraged her to go into any field she wanted to, as long as she graduated from college.

To her father, education was the key to opportunity, as it had certainly proved to be in his own case. Asimiyu ("Sim") Oyetunji received his bachelor's degree in engineering from the University of Maine in the 1960s, and his doctorate from Iowa State University. An engineer for Shell Oil Company in Nigeria, he sent all seven of his children to the U.S. for professional university educations, two of them following in his footsteps at Orono.

"He saw it as a way for us to be something. It was important to be an educated person and be able to provide for ourselves," says Oyetunji. Her father didn't differentiate between his five daughters and two sons, although as the eldest child, she felt her parents placed high expectations on her.

The Nigeria of Oyetunji's youth was wracked by coups and military rule. Born in 1974 in Bonny, Rivers State, she grew up in Lagos relatively unaffected by the political turmoil, attending boarding school and studying math and statistics at a polytechnic university, followed by a one-year internship with a bank. Then it was on to the University of Benin, in Benin City, Nigeria, where she studied pure and applied math for two years. As ever in her studies, she was one of few women. "It wasn't an issue for me, because even in high school, in the last few years you are separated by subject. I was in the science track. I was used to being a minority. All the females bonded well, and also with the boys in the class," she says.

In her early twenties, Oyetunji began delving into her identity. One part was Yoruba, her tribal ancestry. A West African ethnic group with its own language, Yorubas live mostly in western Nigeria, including Lagos.

"The Yoruba part of me was who I was; I never thought about it. It became more important to me later," says Oyetunji. At the time, it was her Muslim identity that she began to explore. She and her siblings had all received religious training, studying the Koran and Arabic, but their parents left it up to them to decide what to do with it. The family prayed and observed religious holy days, but allowed their children to have non-Muslim friends. Their mother wore no hejab.

As a young woman pondering what kind of life she wanted to live, Oyetunji started to express herself in different clothing fashions. While she had formerly dressed Western-style and kept a headscarf in her purse to don when she went to the mosque, she now started to wear more traditional Nigerian clothing with matching headdress. Then, for a time, she added a scarf around her neck, and later added it on to her headdress.

"At that point, I decided to wear Western clothing with hejab. My family were taken aback," she remembers. At her own pace, she had moved through the different styles, with their varying degrees of religious expression, arriving at one that must have seemed conservative to her family and friends. She has worn it ever since. "Once I put that scarf on, it was clear who I was. I wanted to be more spiritual, and be identified as being spiritual," she says.

Around the same time, when Oyetunji was twenty-two, she found herself suddenly at home, along with three of her siblings, with nothing to do. Nigerian universities had shut down amid the country's ongoing political agitation, and it wasn't easy to find a job. So she took a leap of faith onto her father's path by applying to college in Maine. Just before she left home in 1998, she married a Nigerian attorney who had grown up in England and was practicing law in Nigeria; he would join her in Portland in the fall, but that spring, she arrived on the University of Southern Maine campus alone.

Facing Mainers' curiosity about her *hejab* wasn't her only challenge that year. To someone who had never experienced snow, Maine's weather was daunting—especially during the historic ice storm that January. And to a Nigerian brought up in Lagos, Portland seemed small and confining. Africa's second largest city after Cairo, with a metropolitan area population of 8 million, the West African coastal city of Lagos is Nigeria's bustling economic hub and onetime capital city, before the capital was moved to Abuja in 1991. The booming oil industry that has fueled Lagos's hypergrowth and wealth has destabilized the area economically and socially, yet the city retains its vibrant way of life.

Oyetunji's world had shrunk considerably. She carried on without her husband, except for one brief visit from him that November. By spring 2000, he, too, was a USM student, in a graduate program at the Muskie School of Public Service. Oyetunji and her husband, Najim Animashaun, graduated together in 2002—an event attended by their proud families, who were treated like dignitaries as Oyetunji gave her student commencement address. By now, the young couple had a daughter, born in 1999. In this respect, Oyetunji had veered from the path her father had urged her to follow. "He wanted his children to get a bachelor's before marrying. It was much to his chagrin when I got married and even had a child before I graduated," she says.

After graduation, Oyetunji worked as a programmer-analyst at Maine Medical Center for a year, and another daughter was born in 2003. Her husband practiced law in a local firm for a time before joining a United Nations development program that sent him to Afghanistan in 2005. Oyetunji's life grew even busier when she entered an M.B.A. program in USM's business school. Her Maine Medical Center work experience had triggered a desire to go into business. "I wanted to understand the business side of what I was doing," she says. Along with her studies, she worked a short stint at the Maine State Housing Authority, where she trained staff at homeless shelters in using information systems. "It was very humbling for me to work with the homeless," says Oyetunji.

In 2006, she got her M.B.A. Throughout her USM years, she had done extracurricular activities as well, helping raise awareness about diversity and Islam. But those issues took a more personal turn when she spent the summer of 2004 in London and returned to Nigeria for the first time in six years.

"In England, there were Muslims everywhere, and my headdress wasn't such an oddity. That gave me a boost," she says. "I realized that I had become more conservative while living in Portland because most of the Muslims I interacted with were conservative. Leaving Maine made me ask myself, 'Who am I?' In Nigeria, I didn't really fit in any more. I was looking at it through different eyes. 'Where do I belong?' I wondered, questioning things I never questioned before.

"In Nigeria, I came back to who I used to be. Now I'm less conservative," says Oyetunji, who on a more recent visit to Nigeria felt she had come full circle. "Now I feel comfortable in my own skin."

Returning to Maine, she realized that she was forming a desire for a career combining culture with business and identity issues. So she sought advice from her honors professor, Janice Thompson, who guided her through studies in "border identity." Attending a conference in Dubai on women as global leaders and a course in Hong Kong, where Oyetunji learned about Asian business practices and culture, exposed her to more new ideas. Drawing on her Yoruba background of oral storytelling, Oyetunji began interviewing foreign women to document their experiences going through the same identity changes. She describes that transition as a circular process that cannot be completed until a person returns to his or her native country and sees it from a new perspective.

While Oyetunji struggled with her own perspective throughout her student years, she marveled at the often ignorant one Americans expressed about her country. "Someone had seriously asked me if we lived in trees. I said, 'Yes, and the American embassy is in the biggest tree,'" she laughs. She once used the incident as a role-play in a USM conference on diversity that forced her to confront some of her own issues. For example, she had never met anyone who was openly gay before coming to Maine. She examined how she related to gay and lesbian dorm-mates and students with disabilities, and to being seen as a racial minority.

After a decade in Maine, Oyetunji weighs what to her are the positive and negative aspects of American and Nigerian cultural expectations.

"There's a sense of independence here, that children can speak and be listened to and have rights. Things can change quickly here just by my speaking," she says. In Nigeria, making a change involves a long process steeped in traditional respect for one's age and status. On the other hand, she regrets what gets lost in America's "time-is-money" culture.

"People keep to themselves more here. I mourn that," she says. "I was raised in Nigeria to be a strong woman, regardless of people's expectations. You're raised to believe that you should be able to take care of yourself, and you have a lot of women around you who will help you do that. Here you don't have that. I feel lonely because of that." Still, in Maine she found a small, friendly environment where she was able to connect with other people, get jobs, and practice skills more easily than she could have in a big city, she believes. Now she has reached a point where she wants to get a Ph.D. and explore the world.

"Because my interest is global, I want to be in a place that is global. Since my husband went to Afghanistan, we're even more global. I've spent about one-third of my life here. It's time for me to leave. But Maine will always be part of me; I'll always come here," says Oyetunji. Among other strong connections to the state, her two sisters who graduated from UMO work as engineers in Auburn and are married to white Mainers who converted to Islam. Eventually, she would like to do research and teach, or work for an international nonprofit organization. In the meantime, she is setting up a Nigerian nonprofit to advise Muslim women about starting businesses.

"My spirituality keeps me grounded. No matter what my path is, whatever is good for me is what will happen to me," says Oyetunji. Having recently become more aware of her mortality after the loss of several close friends, she is more conscious than ever of wanting to leave a legacy for others, including her own children, when she is gone: "I want my daughters to know it's okay for a Muslim woman, with or without a headdress, to do whatever she wants to do."

A Look at Recent Immigration in Maine

Each year, Maine people encounter a greater variety of foreign-born doctors, professors, engineers, and social-service professionals, discover new ethnic groceries and restaurants, attend a wider array of cross-cultural events, and hire immigrant workers from more countries. In certain parts of the state, primarily its largest cities, this new diversity has had a dramatic impact since the recent wave of new types of immigrants started coming to Maine about thirty years ago. In Portland's public schools, for example, students speak fifty different languages.

What is striking about Maine's recent immigration is not the overall numbers of newcomers, but rather how extremely diverse they are, coming from all over the globe—in contrast to, say, southwestern states whose immigrant population comes largely from Latin America.

As the state with the oldest population in the U.S., due mainly to a loss of young people to other parts of the country, Maine has reason to cheer the arrival of these immigrants. They play a big part in revitalizing our communities.

Who Are the New Mainers?

In our very broad, nonlegal definition of immigrants, the new Mainers are people who have come to the state from other countries. Among the people profiled in this book are refugees, green-card holders, temporary workers with special visas, and a migrant worker. Some are U.S. citizens, some not. Typically, about two-thirds of all legal immigrants to this country come through family sponsorship.[1] The remainder are divided fairly equally between refugees and people who come on work visas or employment programs.

While a walk down a street in downtown Portland or Lewiston may leave an impression of a state with widespread diversity, in fact the opposite is true. Maine is the whitest state in America, along with Vermont.[2] A 2006 U.S. Census Bureau estimate reported that Maine had only about 42,000 foreign-born residents, or just 3.2 percent of its population of 1.3 million, ranking it forty-second among all the states.

"Foreign-born" means anyone who is not a U.S. citizen at birth. (Agencies dealing with immigrants stress that they are undercounted in census data because many are reluctant to report to the U.S. Census Bureau.) The Immigrant Legal Advocacy Project (ILAP) in Portland estimates that more than 50,000 immigrants from over 100 countries have moved to the state since the early 1980s.

Furthermore, Maine's foreign-born population only rose by 14.3 percent between 2000 and 2006, one of the lowest growth rates in the U.S., according to the Migration Policy Institute, which compiles census and other survey data. Maine experienced an immigration surge in the 1990s, when the economy was booming and unemployment was low; immigrants saw Maine as safer and cheaper to live in than other states. Since then, the growth rate has slowed, according to ILAP.

No one knows how many undocumented immigrants live in Maine, but most estimates put the number at more than 5,000. According to immigrant advocates, that population started to shrink in 2007 as Hispanics began leaving due to racial profiling by police.[3] A law passed by Maine's Legislature in 2008 requiring residents to prove their immigration status in order to get a driver's license is expected to exacerbate that trend.

Whereas in many other parts of the country, immigration is helping local economies by offsetting the loss of traditional residents, the lower rates of immigration to Maine and other northern New England states is causing the region to grow more slowly than the U.S. as a whole. Maine is perceived as remote geographically, far away from certain sources of labor such as Mexico, and cold, with a short season for migrant workers.

Observers seeing Africans walking Portland's or Lewiston's streets in colorful, flowing garb in recent years may hold an impression of large numbers of African immigrants changing the demographics of Maine. But it turns out that Africans made up only 11 percent of all foreign-born people living in Maine as of 2006. North Americans (primarily Canadians) made up the largest share, almost one-third, with the next largest group, a little over one-quarter, coming from Europe. The remaining immigrants included Asians (21 percent), Latin Americans (9 percent), and a few from Oceania (0.6 percent).[4]

REFUGEES

The most visible of Maine's recent immigrants are refugees. Some were sent to the state directly, usually from refugee camps in intermediary countries. A greater number moved here after initially being resettled somewhere else in the U.S. And some were granted asylum from persecution once they were already here.

Because the refugees from Africa and Southeast Asia stand out in the state's overwhelmingly white population, it may seem that Maine has laid out a bigger welcome mat than it really has. In fact, Maine resettles one of the smallest numbers of refugees of anyplace in the U.S., and fewer in the past few years than it used to. In 2007, the state resettled only 118 refugees—ninety-four from Somalia and the rest from Sudan, Iran, Democratic Republic of Congo, Ethiopia, Burma, and Vietnam—about half what it once did, according to the U.S. Office of Refugee Resettlement.

The numbers of refugees may be low, but they represent one of the most diverse groups in America. For example, from 1981 to 2004, nearly 5,000 "primary" refugees (those who came directly from abroad) arrived from more than thirty countries, including Cambodia, Vietnam, Bosnia, Sudan, Russia, Somalia, Poland, Afghanistan, Iran, and Ethiopia, according to Catholic Charities Maine's Refugee and Immigration Services. Like other refugees, those interviewed for this book suffered persecution of one kind or another and endured extreme physical and/or mental hardship. Most survived civil wars. Many waited years in appalling refugee camps before coming here.

A lot of people wonder why refugees from climates and cultures so different from Maine's get sent here. The answer lies in a complex cooperation among the United Nations, the U.S. State Department, and nongovernmental voluntary agencies. Initially, the Office of the UN High Commissioner for Refugees determines refugees' status and works to place them in certain countries—a process that can take many years. The president and Congress set the number of refugees to be admitted into the U.S. annually, and there are also limits by global geographic regions.

Refugees may be offered a choice of a few different countries, but may not get their first choice. The refugees who selected Maine typically chose it based on word-of-mouth stories of a quiet, safe place to raise a family.

The U.S. State Department assigns refugees to American nonprofit agencies, which in turn assign them to their local affiliates, who then choose placement in communities believed to be welcoming. Unlike other states, Maine has only one such agency, Catholic Charities Maine. In the past thirty years, it has settled more than 12,000 refugees of all types into their new lives, providing housing, furnishings, food, clothing, and modest financial support for their first thirty days here.[5] They can also use services such as community-orientation, English-language training, job-placement, and mental-health programs for ninety days.

SECONDARY MIGRANTS

By far the greatest majority of Maine's immigrants—perhaps as many as 80 percent—are believed to be "secondary migrants," many of whom started moving to Maine in 2000 from other places in the country to join family members or to escape cities they found too big and unsafe for their families. "Secondary migrant" is a legal term referring to refugees who are resettled in one location in the U.S. and who move during their first eight months in the country, when their resettlement benefits can follow them. Refugees who relocate to Maine after that time period lose their benefits.

Agencies who work with secondary migrants

are seeing more arrivals all the time, coming from nearby cities like Boston or sites as far away as California, Texas, and Georgia. For instance, the city of Portland's Refugee Services Program, which has primarily served secondary migrants since 2000, saw a jump in new clients from an average of 400 a year in 2003-2006, to 668 in 2007. The majority were Somali, with others coming from Sudan, Rwanda, Congo/Zaire, Iraq, Afghanistan, Djibouti, and Ethiopia.[6]

A broader definition of secondary migrants includes non-refugees—immigrants who are mainly employment-based workers, who tend to be highly skilled and educated. It is almost impossible to determine precisely how many secondary migrants of all types live in Maine, since they move into (or out of) the state the same as native-born Americans do.

MIGRANT WORKERS
Migrant workers are essential to Maine's economy, taking jobs others won't. For instance, in agriculture, forestry, and the hospitality industry, more than 90 percent of the workers are foreign born, according to the Maine Department of Labor. Hispanic and Southeast Asian seasonal migrant workers work from May through October planting and harvesting trees, or working for growers of potatoes, blueberries, apples, broccoli, eggs, and maple syrup. Others work through the winter in wreath-making and seafood-processing.

At the peak of the growing season, anywhere from 8,000 to 12,000 seasonal farm workers live in Maine, a number that has grown constantly since the 1980s. But as more and more Hispanics leave, under pressure from police harassment and the national political climate on immigration, employers complain that they can't find enough workers. Like other American growers, Maine's saw about one-third of their crops go unharvested in 2007.[7]

Some migrant workers come from abroad with temporary agricultural-worker visas arranged by their employers. Others already live in Maine and follow the harvests. In the past few

years, hundreds of Canadian loggers have crossed the border to work in Maine's northern forests. Workers from much farther away work there, too. In 2002, fourteen Honduran and Guatemalan workers died in a van accident as they commuted to their work site. Some former construction workers have shifted to other seasonal jobs due to the recent economic downturn affecting the construction industry.

WHERE ARE THE IMMIGRANTS SETTLING?
The greatest concentration of new immigrants is in Portland, where they have boosted population in a city that has been losing residents. In the 1990s, the number of foreign-born residents increased almost 50 percent to 4,895, making up a 7.6 percent share of the city's population of a little over 64,000 in the 2000 U.S. Census, while the native-born population declined almost 3 percent. About 10 percent of city residents spoke a language other than English at home that year, the last for which census data are available.

Arriving immigrants are also balancing a population decline in Lewiston, where mill closings have driven out thousands of residents. Maine's second largest city drew national attention for its influx of Somalis starting in 2001. By now, more than 3,500 Somalis live in Lewiston, a city of about 37,000—almost all of them secondary migrants who moved there for affordable housing, jobs and a safer, healthier quality of life than they found in big cities like Atlanta.[8]

Significant numbers of refugees and secondary migrants have also settled in the smaller communities of Biddeford, Saco, Gorham, Sanford, South Portland, and Westbrook.

HOW ARE IMMIGRANTS CHANGING MAINE?
Mainers have reason to be thankful to its new immigrant families, since their numbers are helping make up for an aging population with a significant decline in young people in the workforce. In fact, Maine is the "oldest" state in the country, with the highest median age.[9] In 2007, Maine showed one of the lowest population

growth rates in the nation, partly because it didn't get as much immigration as other parts of the country.[10] Since businesses seek locations with solid supplies of workers and a growing market, the state needs to add population to revitalize a lagging economy.

However, only 3.4 percent of Maine's civilian employed workforce was foreign born in 2006, ranking it forty-fifth among all states. Furthermore, more than half of Maine's foreign-born workers were from Northern America (largely Canada) and Europe, in stark contrast to the rest of the country, where workers from Latin America make up more than half, according to the Migration Policy Institute.

Many people picture immigrants working at entry-level jobs such as assembly-line positions. That is true for refugees. For instance, the city of Portland's Refugee Services Program placed clients recently in entry-level jobs at area employers such as Aramark, a food services company; Barber Foods, a chicken-processing factory; Granite Bay Care, a human-services agency; and Maine Medical Center.

But the vast majority of other foreign-born workers in Maine work in management, professional, sales and office, and service occupations, in the fields of education, health care, and social assistance; manufacturing; and retail trade, according to the Migration Policy Institute. Maine has few people of color working in its professional class. African and Asian refugees complain that they find almost no people who look like them when they walk into offices, and see few role models for their children, many of whom wind up leaving the state for jobs.[11]

Finally, immigrants contribute to the state's economy by opening their own businesses. The most visible are the great numbers of ethnic restaurants popping up around the state in the past few decades. Others include cleaning, landscape services, construction and construction-related companies, many of them started by Hispanics and Southeast Asians; and stores, arts enterprises, and social-services agencies.

New Mainers have changed the state's education picture, too. When it comes to higher education, the achievement of Maine's immigrants outshines other residents and shows a steady climb. More than one-third of the foreign-born population had a college degree in 2006, compared to only about one-quarter in Maine's and the nation's native-born population, according to the Migration Policy Institute. International students who wind up staying in the state after college bring their perspectives to local communities. In the public schools, immigrant students have expanded native-born students' knowledge of the world not only by their presence in class and on sports teams, but through diversity clubs and other social activities furthering cross-cultural education.

Recent immigrants have taught Maine residents a lot about their cultures, tying us to the rest of the world in new ways. Whether through music and dance performances or community activism or public discussions or writing newspaper columns, they have offered Mainers a multicultural public education unparalleled in the state's history. Virtually all the immigrant groups have organizations whose members actively participate in the civic life of the state; and informally, as immigrants meet their native-born neighbors, cultural bridges are crossed.

MAINE'S RESPONSE

Mainers' reaction to recent immigrants has been mixed. Despite a few well-publicized incidents of racist behavior, most native-born Mainers genuinely embrace the greater diversity, cultural excitement, and skills the immigrants bring, and can often be heard expressing admiration for their new neighbors from far away.

New Mainers praise the state for its welcoming people. There have been problems, for sure, particularly for Africans and Latinos. Lewiston made national headlines in 2002 when the then-mayor asked Somalis to stop coming to the city because services were overwhelmed, and again in 2006 when a man threw a pig's head into a mosque. But in both cases, local citizens rallied on Somalis' behalf. Some native-born Mainers display bigotry, but not more than in other states, say the immigrants.

In Portland and Lewiston, Africans and Asians have complained for years that the police unfairly target them. And throughout the state, Latinos report unwarranted stops by police who ask their immigration status—a problem they consider worse in Maine than in states with more diverse populations because Latinos stand out in Maine's overwhelmingly white population.

Overall, though, Maine has responded warmly to unprecedented challenges, for example, creating a new state Office of Multicultural Affairs a few years ago and developing programs such as a New Mainers Partnership between Portland and Lewiston, Catholic Charities Maine, and the Training Resource Center to offer secondary migrants case-management services. In a state with close, informal relationships among agencies, such partnerships have mobilized more quickly than in states with larger populations— a fact reflected in immigrants' comments that they receive good social services here.

In Lewiston, for instance, the public schools, federal and nonprofit agencies, churches, local Somali groups, an Islamic Center, the Center for the Prevention of Hate Violence, local colleges, the housing authority, the labor department, and numerous volunteer organizations are just some of the many entities that have come together in just a few short years to meet the needs of secondary migrants.

The public schools and University of Maine System have scrambled to meet the needs of English-language learners. Students in Portland's public schools speak some fifty different languages, an extraordinary diversity unmatched in most of the country. Whereas many schools around the U.S. have bilingual programs, Portland has a multilingual program teaching English as a Second Language. Begun in 1980 with about fifty students from Southeast Asia, the program has grown to around 1,500 students, or about one-fifth of the district's enrollment.[12] The school district has attracted numerous federal grants and been awarded the national

designation "program of academic excellence."

Adult-education programs have also geared up their ESL classes to meet new demands. Portland's upsurge began in the 1970s with the arrival of Southeast Asian refugees. The numbers grew from about 400 students in 1995 to more than 1,000 from over sixty countries in 2007. With a combination of local, state, and federal funding, almost all the program's classes are free for learners.[13] Adult education programs in Portland and Lewiston offer survival, citizenship, and GED ESL classes.

Outside of Portland and a handful of other cities in southern Maine, the numbers of ESL students remains low, however. Given the high media profile of Portland schools with many refugee pupils, it is surprising to learn that the "limited English proficient" population of Maine as a whole only increased by about one-third from 2000 to 2006, half the change occurring nationally.

Many Maine employers have reached out to recent immigrant workers. Certain employers around the state not only hire immigrants, but also, like Barber Foods in Portland, offer free classes for employees. The Diversity Hiring Coalition of Maine, a group of schools, businesses, and nonprofit organizations, works on boosting workplace diversity.

Churches, synagogues, and mosques have played a large role in helping integrate immigrants into Maine's way of life. And thousands of native-born Mainers volunteer to help immigrants, or reach out as friends. For a state not known for its welcome to "people from away," Maine gets high marks from its most recent immigrants.

For more information about Maine's immigrants and a complete list of resources, please see the Maine Department of Health and Human Services/Office of Multicultural Resources website: www.maine.gov/dhhs/oma/Multicultural Resource/intro.html

1. "Multicultural Resources—Introduction to Immigration," *Maine Department of Health and Human Services/Office of Multicultural Resources, 2007,* www.maine.gov/dhhs/oma/Multicultural Resource/intro.html, 8 August 2008.

2. Maine alternated with Vermont from 2003 to 2006 (the last date for which figures were available) as the state with the highest percentage of white residents. U.S. Census Bureau, "United States and States: Percentage of the Population Who Are White Alone," *2006 American Community Survey,* http://factfinder.census.gov, 8 August 2008.

3. Beth Stickney, executive director, Immigrant Legal Advocacy Project, telephone interview by author, 7 August 2008; and Juan Perez-Febles, director & monitor advocate, Migrant & Immigrant Services, Maine Department of Labor, telephone interview by author, 11 August 2008.

4. Migration Policy Institute, "Fact Sheet on the Foreign Born," *MPI Data Hub,* 2008, www.migrationinformation.org/datahub, 8 August 2008.

5. "Multicultural Resources—Introduction to Immigration," *Maine Department of Health and Human Services/Office of Multicultural Resources,* 2007, www.maine.gov/dhhs/oma/Multicultural Resource/intro.html, 8 August 2008.

6. Robert Duranleau and Regina Phillips, "Refugee Services Program Year-End Report, FY 2007," *City of Portland, Health and Human Services Department, Social Services Division.*

7. Juan Perez-Febles, director and monitor advocate, Migrant and Immigrant Services, Maine Department of Labor, telephone interview by author, 11 August 2008.

8. Phil Nadeau, deputy city administrator, City of Lewiston, e-mail communication with the author, 11 August 2008.

9. U.S. Census Bureau, "Maine in Focus: Census Bureau Pre-Caucus Snapshot," 31 January 2008, www.census.gov/PressRelease/ www/releases/archives/voting/011434.html, 8 August 2008.

10. Bret Schulte, "New Census Data Shows Northeast Population Growth is Lagging," *U.S. News & World Report,* 26 March 2008.

11. Trevor Maxwell, "A White Professional Class," *Portland Press Herald/Maine Sunday Telegram,* 21 November 2005.

12. Grace Valenzuela, director, Portland Public Schools Multilingual and Multicultural Center, e-mail communication with the author, 13 August 2008.

13. Robert Wood, co-director, Portland Adult Education, e-mail communication with the author, 13 August 2008.

ABOUT THE AUTHORS

Photographer Jan Pieter van Voorst van Beest is a Dutch national who moved to Maine from the Netherlands in 1970. His work has been widely shown in solo, group, and juried exhibits in the U.S and Holland. He has published three books of photography: *San Miguel de Allende*, a photographic essay; *Portland, Maine, in Black and White*; and *Flesh and Stone*. He started in photography in the early 1970s after taking courses at the Portland School of Art, now the Maine College of Art. He also had a long career as a transportation and logistics executive.

Pat Nyhan wrote the text for this book. She is a former journalist with the *Portland Press Herald/Maine Sunday Telegram* and *Maine Times* who teaches English as a Second Language to immigrants. She has worked for Human Rights Watch on African issues, taught English in Afghanistan in the Peace Corps, and taught media studies at the University of Southern Maine. The author of *Zigzag: A Working Woman's Life in Changing Times* and *Let the Good Times Roll! A Guide to Cajun & Zydeco Music*, Pat has lived in Maine for almost thirty years.

Reza Jalali, who wrote the book's foreword, is a writer and community organizer. Originally from Iran, he has lived in Maine for over two decades. A refugee and human-rights advocate who has visited many refugee camps, he speaks nationally on Islam, the Middle East, and refugee and human-rights issues, and leads workshops on cultural diversity. Jalali, who holds an M.F.A., teaches at the University of Southern Maine, where he also manages the Office of Multicultural Student Affairs.